Key skills for kids
READING AND WRITING

Let's get started!

priddy books
big ideas for little people

Contents

Answers are on pages 118–127!

Write letters A–M

There are 26 letters in the alphabet. Each letter has **uppercase** and **lowercase** forms.

1 Trace and write the uppercase and lowercase letters.

A A A	**a** a a
B B B	**b** b b
C C C	**c** c c
D D D	**d** d d
E E E	**e** e e

F F F   f f f

G G G   g g g

H H H   h h h

I I I   i i i

J J J   j j j

K K K   k k k

L L L   l l l

M M M   m m m

Can you think of any words that begin with these letters?

1 Trace and write the uppercase and lowercase letters.

N N N	n n n
O O O	o o o
P P P	p p p
Q Q Q	q q q
R R R	r r r

S s s

s s s

T t t

t t t

U u u

U u u

V v v

V v v

W w w

W w w

X x x

X x x

Y y y

y y y

Z z z

z z z

Nature abc

| b | | d | e | | g | |

| j | | m | | o | p | |

| s | | u | | w | x | |

2 Following the example, write the words in **alphabetical order** on the lines below.

moth   ant   snail   bee

1. ....ant............

2. ....

3. ....

4. ....

Use the first letter of each word to help put them in abc order.

All about me

1 Write your first name and last name. Then draw a picture of yourself in the frame.

Don't forget to use an uppercase letter for the first letter of your first name and your last name.

My name is

....

....

2 Answer each question.

My favorite food is

....

My favorite color is

....

My birthday is in the month of

....

Days of the week

There are seven days in a week.

Days of the week always start with a **capital letter**.

1 Read the days of the week aloud.

| Sunday | Monday | Tuesday |

| Wednesday | Thursday | Friday | Saturday |

2 Following the example, write which day comes next.

Tuesday / Wednesday / Thursday ....Friday..........

Sunday / Monday / Tuesday ....

Thursday / Friday / Saturday ....

3 Fill in the chart with the correct days of the week.

Yesterday	Today	Tomorrow
Tuesday	Wednesday	
	Monday	
	Sunday	
	Thursday	

Adam's diary

Adam does a different activity on each day of the week.

Monday	Tuesday	Wednesday	Thursday	Friday
Swim lesson	Piano lesson	Park	Soccer game	Party

1 Which day does Adam do each activity? Write the day in the correct place in the crossword.

Use the pictures to help you!

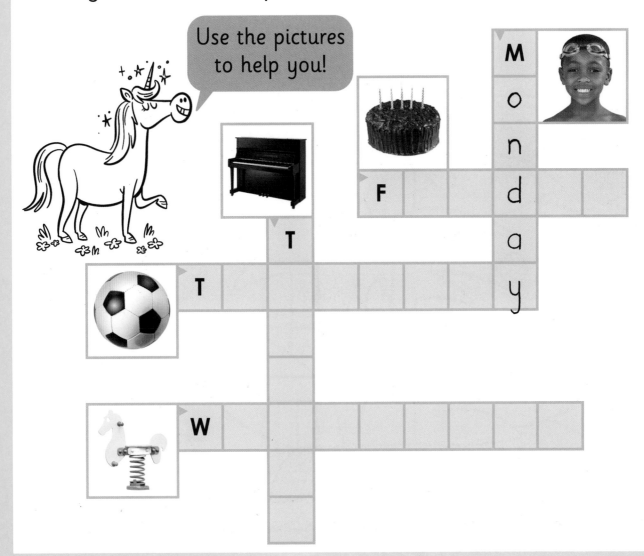

What is "I?"

"I" can be a letter or a word.

Always use a **capital letter** when writing "I" as a word.

1 Read the text.
Circle the word "**I**" in each sentence.

I like bears.
I like parrots.
I like monkeys.
I do not like snakes!

2 Color the word "**I**" pink.
Color the word "**me**" green.

Characters

Characters are the people, animals, or creatures in a story.

1 Put an **X** next to the pictures that are characters.

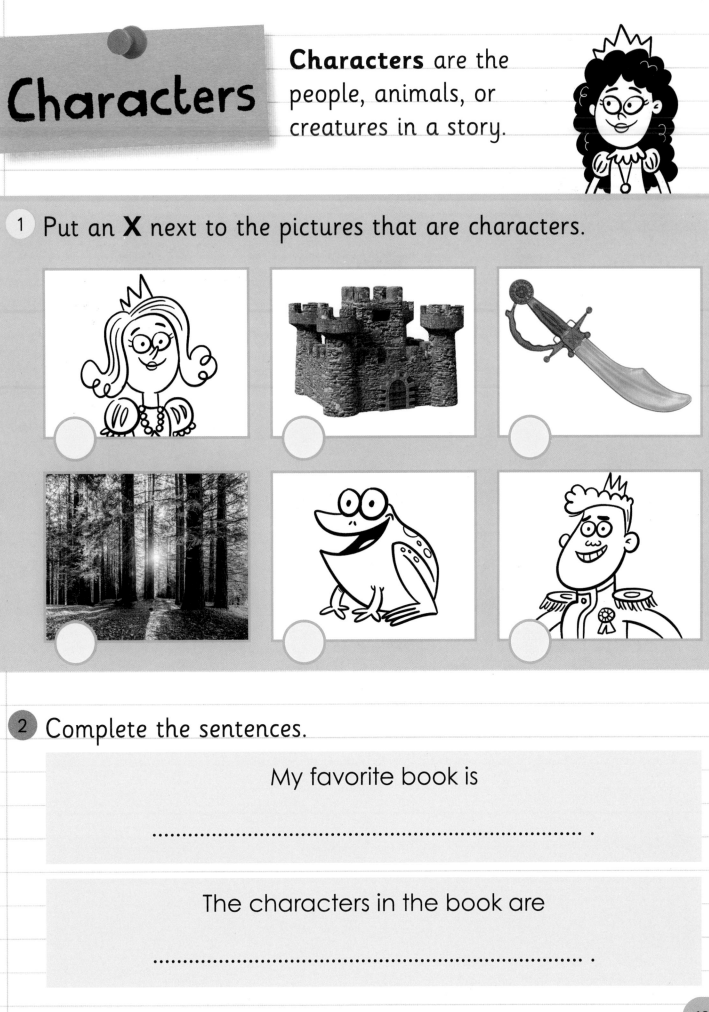

2 Complete the sentences.

My favorite book is

....

The characters in the book are

....

Create a character

Every story has a **main character**. The main character is the person or animal that the story is mostly about.

1 Create a character by filling in the blanks.

Argh! I'm Captain Toby, a scary pirate.

My character's name is ....
My character lives in ....
My character likes to ....

2 Circle three words that describe your character.

| kind | noisy | bossy | brave | clumsy |

| happy | wild | loving | shy | funny |

3 Draw a picture of your character, then write their description.

....
....
....
....
....
....

Compare characters

Compare means to find things that are similar or different.

Readers can compare characters in a story.

1 Read the story below.

Tom and May sat down to eat lunch.

Tom opened his lunch box. "Yes, I love my lunch!"

May opened her lunch box. "Oh no!" she said.

Tom started to eat his fruit. He saw that May was sad.

"Do you want some grapes?" he asked.

May smiled. "Yes, please," she said.

"I have strawberries, but I don't

like them." "I like strawberries!" said Tom.

May and Tom shared their grapes

and strawberries.

2 Check the correct boxes for each character.

	May	Tom
Likes strawberries		
Does not like strawberries		
Shares lunch with a friend		

Setting

A **setting** is where and when a story takes place.

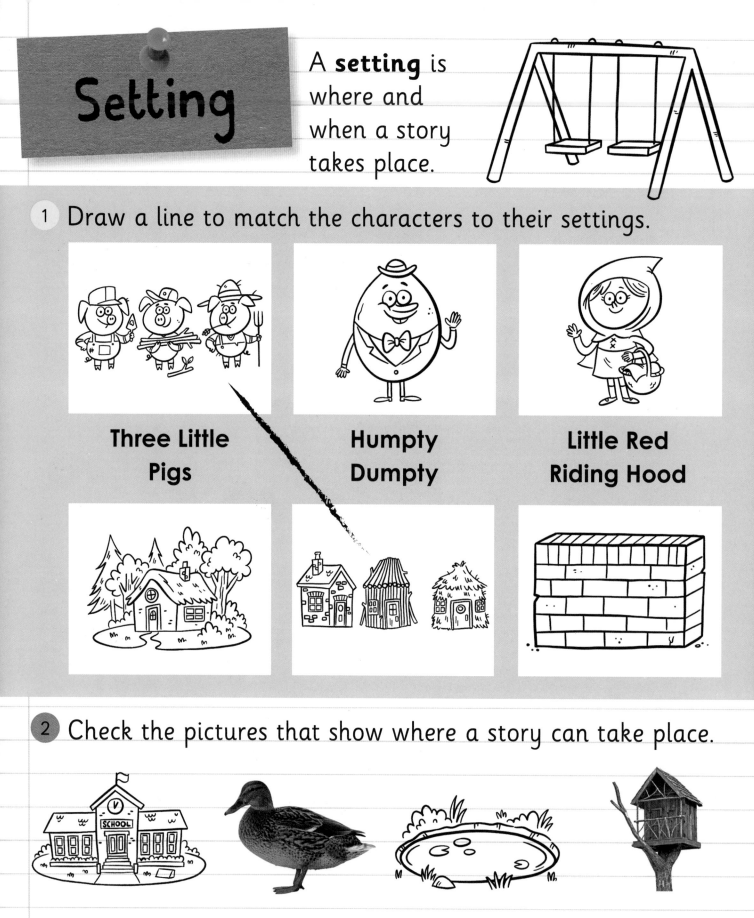

1 Draw a line to match the characters to their settings.

Three Little Pigs

Humpty Dumpty

Little Red Riding Hood

2 Check the pictures that show where a story can take place.

school

duck

pond

tree house

Characters and setting

The **characters** and **setting** are details that help readers understand the story.

1 Read the story. Then circle the character names.

> Goose and Duck are best friends. They live in the same pond.
> They love to play together every day.
> One day, Goose and Duck saw black dots by their pond.
> The next day the black dots were gone!
> Lots of new frog friends had come to live and play with them.

2 Can you label the characters in the picture?

Label means to write the word next to the picture that relates to it.

3 What is the setting of the story? ....

Capital letters

Days, months, and names begin with a capital letter.

Capital letters are used to start a sentence.

① Underline the words that need a capital letter.

december	sunday	john	dog
car	august	jump	mary

② Circle the capital letters in each sentence.

a. We jumped so high.

b. My best friend is Cleo.

c. No way!

d. Are you going to play basketball on Friday?

③ Write out each sentence with capital letters in the correct places.

a. the kangaroo loves to jump.

....

Hello, I'm Hopper!

b. his name is hopper.

....

c. can you jump higher than he can?

....?

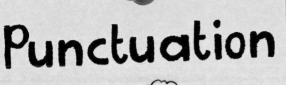

Punctuation

Every sentence ends with a **punctuation** mark. Most sentences end with a **period**. A question ends with a **question mark**. An exclamation ends with an **exclamation point**.

1 Draw a line from each punctuation mark to its name.

?	**!**	**.**

exclamation point	period	question mark

2 Place a check next to the sentence with correct punctuation.

period

☐ I am. seven years old

☐ My name is Harvey.

An **exclamation** is a sentence that shows strong feelings or excitement.

question mark

☐ Where is the party?

☐ Can you teach me ? how to play

exclamation point

☐ Happy birthday!

☐ ! Wow

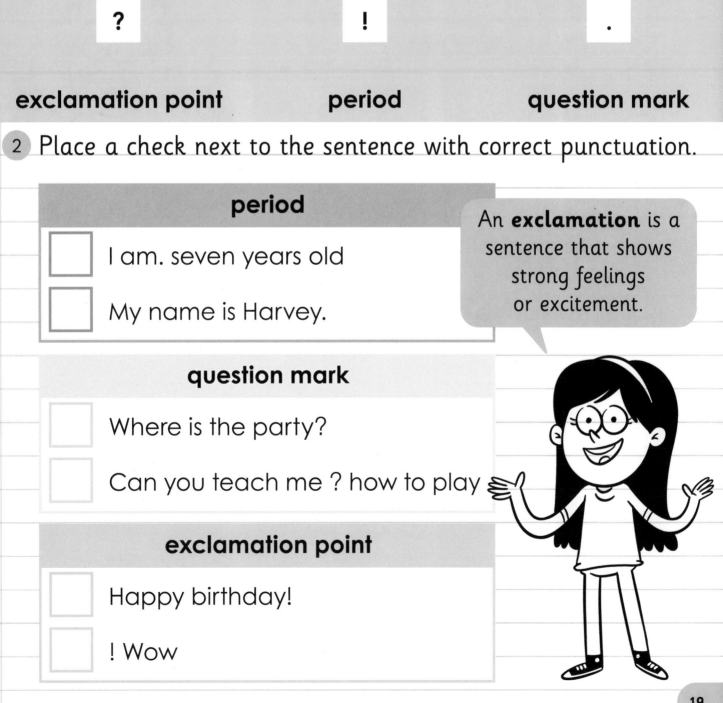

Use punctuation

1 Add the correct punctuation mark to the end of each sentence.

Remember to use a **.** **?** or **!**

a. We like to play soccer ......

b. Where is your cat ......

c. This is so exciting ......

d. What is your favorite color ......

e. Watch out for the swing ......

f. I can climb the tree ......

2 Write the words below in order so that the sentence makes sense.

many	?	kittens	How	do	have	you

....

Sentences

Sentences begin with a capital letter and end with a punctuation mark.

1 Rewrite each sentence using a capital letter and a **.** **?** or **!**

a. can you juggle ....

b. i want a red balloon ....

c. oh no ....

2 Write two sentences about the picture.

1. ....
   ....
   ....
   ....
2. ....
   ....
   ....
   ....

Use a capital letter at the beginning and a **.** **?** or **!** at the end of each sentence.

Beginning sounds

A **beginning sound** is the first sound heard in a word.

1 Write the beginning sound for each of the pictures below.

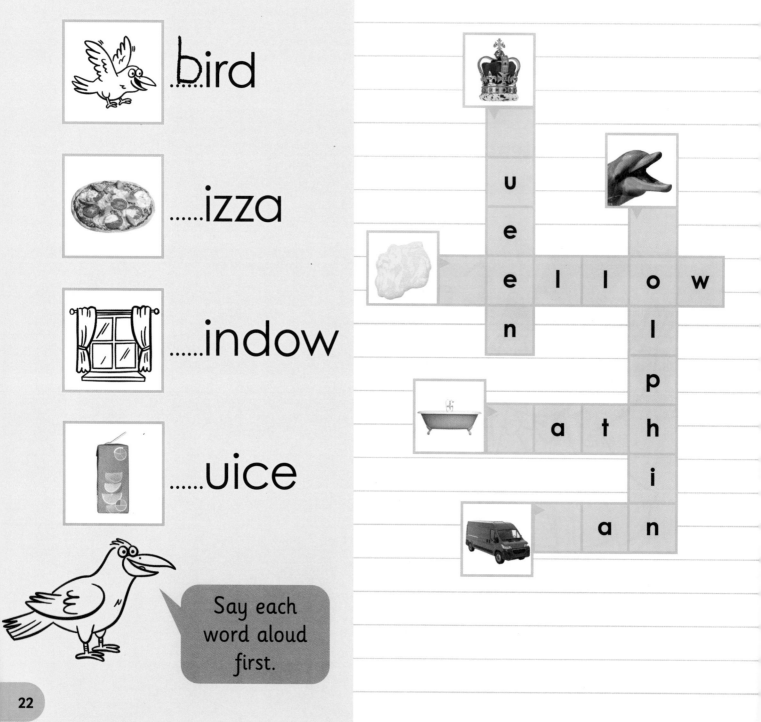

.b.ird

.....izza

.....indow

.....uice

Say each word aloud first.

2 Complete the crossword puzzle by writing the beginning sounds.

u
e
e l l o w
n   l
         p
    a t h
         i
    a n

Ending sounds

An **ending sound** is the last sound heard in a word.

1 Circle the correct ending sound for each of the pictures.

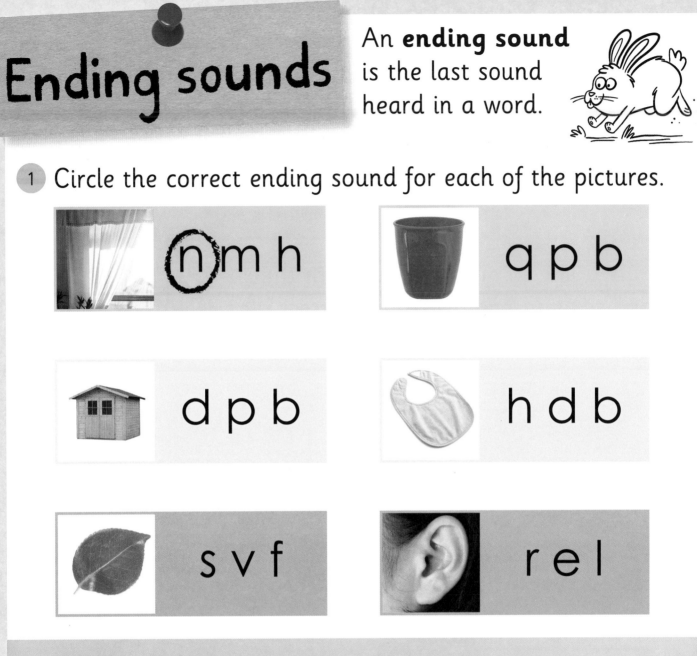

(n) m h

q p b

d p b

h d b

s v f

r e l

---

2 Write the ending sound for each of the pictures below.

lam......

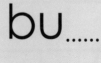
bu......

ne......

gir......

Spelling patterns

A **spelling pattern** is a group of letters that make a special sound when they are put together.

Spelling patterns are sometimes called **word families**.

1 Draw a line to match words with the "**ag**" spelling pattern to the correct picture.

| flag | bag | wag |

2 Finish writing each word with the "**an**" spelling pattern.

m.............

p.............

f ....

r ....

3 The words below have an "**ell**" or "**ill**" spelling pattern. Read each word aloud.

ill

shell

bell

hill

spill

drill

well

yell

4 Put each word from Activity 3 into the correct group.

"ell"	"ill"
....	....
....	....
....	....
....	....

More spelling patterns

1 Circle the words with the "**op**" spelling pattern.

Spelling patterns can help you spell new words.

bed   (stop)   pop

mop   clock   hop

2 Use the "**ug**" spelling pattern to write the words.

r ....   b ....

m ....   j ....

3 Choose an "**ug**" word from the word bank to fill in the gaps.

1. Miles pulled the .... out of the sink.

2. Natalie .... a hole in the sand.

Word bank

dug
plug

Look at the picture

Pictures give a clue about what is happening in the story.

Pictures can also be called **illustrations**.

1 Look at the picture.
Write a story about what is happening in the picture.

....
....
....
....
....
....
....

2 Read the beginning of the story below. Draw a picture to match.

Anna is excited to be at the fair.
She can't wait to go on the fast ride.

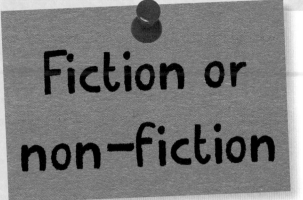

Fiction or non-fiction

Fiction texts are make-believe, or not true. **Non-fiction** texts are true. They give information.

1 Read the title of each book. Draw a line to show whether it is a fiction or non-fiction text.

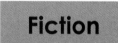 **Fiction**   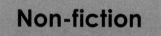 **Non-fiction**

2 Read the sentences.
Write **F** next to the sentences from a fiction text.
Write **N** next to the sentences from a non-fiction text.

a. The monster jumped on the bed. ☐

b. Bees have six legs. ☐

c. Animals need food and water to survive. ☐

d. The princess kissed the frog. ☐

Key details

Key details are important pieces of information in a text.

1 Read the text about the life cycle of a frog.

A frog lays tiny eggs in the water.

After a few weeks, tadpoles hatch from the eggs.

Tadpoles look like little fish with long tails.

These tails help the tadpoles swim.

When tadpoles grow back and front legs, they are called froglets. Froglets look like little frogs with tails. As the froglets grow, their tails become shorter and shorter.

Finally, froglets become adult frogs.

2 Label the life cycle of a frog by choosing the correct word.

frog	froglet	eggs	tadpole

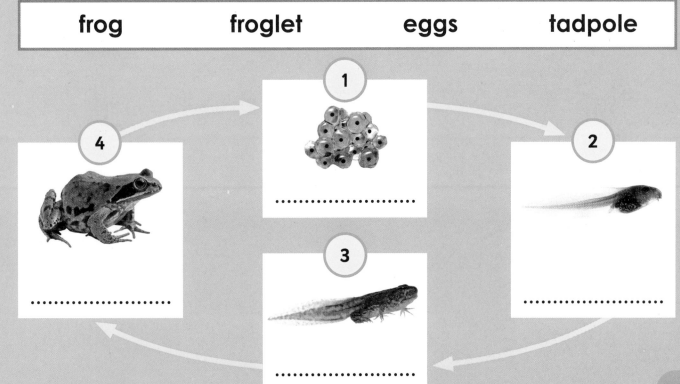

Sequence events

Sequence events means to put different parts of a story in order of when they happen.

1 Read the story.

On Sunday, it was hot outside. Dad took me
to the park. We took my dog, Chip, with us.
I got strawberry ice cream.
When Chip saw a squirrel, he started to run away.
I jumped and my ice cream fell! I was sad.
Then Dad shared his chocolate ice cream with me.

2 Put the story in the correct order by writing
1, 2, or 3 in the boxes.

3 Cross out the word that does not describe
the setting of the story.

outside   park   car   Sunday

Short vowel "a"

Vowels can make many sounds. The same letter can sound long or short, depending on the word that it is in.

The short "a" vowel sounds like /a/ in the word "**cat**."

1 Say each word aloud. Fill in the space with the vowel "**a**." Then write each word.

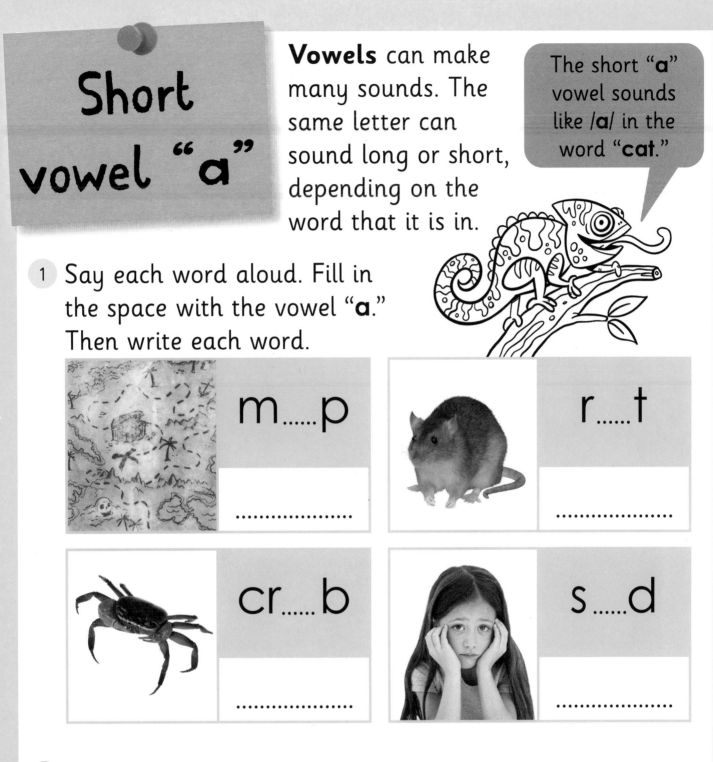

m.....p

r.....t

cr.....b

s.....d

2 Read each word aloud.
Circle the words that have the short "**a**" sound.

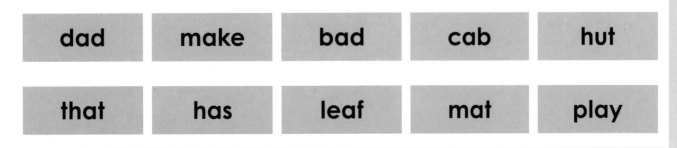

dad	make	bad	cab	hut
that	has	leaf	mat	play

Short vowel "e"

The short "e" vowel sounds like /e/ in the word "**bed**."

1 Say each word aloud. Fill in the space with the vowel "**e**." Then write each word.

10 t......n

....

n......st

....

r......d

....

p......n

....

2 Read each word aloud. Draw a line from the words that have a short "**e**" sound to the circle.

bed   short "e"   vest

get   we

bee   men

yes   tree

Short vowel "i"

1 Read each word with the short "i" sound.
Then write each word under its matching picture.

six	fish	pig	twins

....

2 Read each word aloud.
Place a check next to the words with the short "i" sound.

☐ **big**   ☐ **like**   ☐ **lip**

☐ **fin**   ☐ **kite**   ☐ **his**

☐ **hi**   ☐ **win**   ☐ **bike**

Short vowel "o"

The short "o" vowel sounds like /o/ in the word "hot."

1 Read each short "o" word aloud.
   Write each word under the correct picture.

box	stop	sock

....

2 Draw a line from each short "o" word to the correct picture.

fox

log

jog

dog

Short vowel "u"

The short "u" vowel sounds like /u/ in the word "**bug**."

1 Unscramble the letters to make a word with the short "u" sound.

t c u

....

u c p

....

t u n

....

u g h

....

2 Find the short "u" words in the word search.

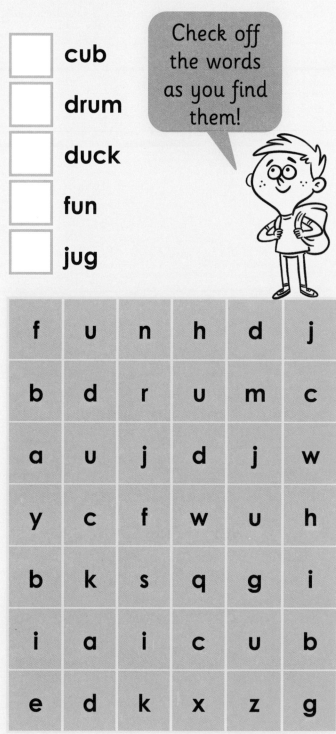

- [ ] **cub**
- [ ] **drum**
- [ ] **duck**
- [ ] **fun**
- [ ] **jug**

Check off the words as you find them!

f	u	n	h	d	j
b	d	r	u	m	c
a	u	j	d	j	w
y	c	f	w	u	h
b	k	s	q	g	i
i	a	i	c	u	b
e	d	k	x	z	g

More short vowels

1 Write the correct short vowel sound to complete the words.

Remember the short vowels are "a," "e," "i," "o," and "u."

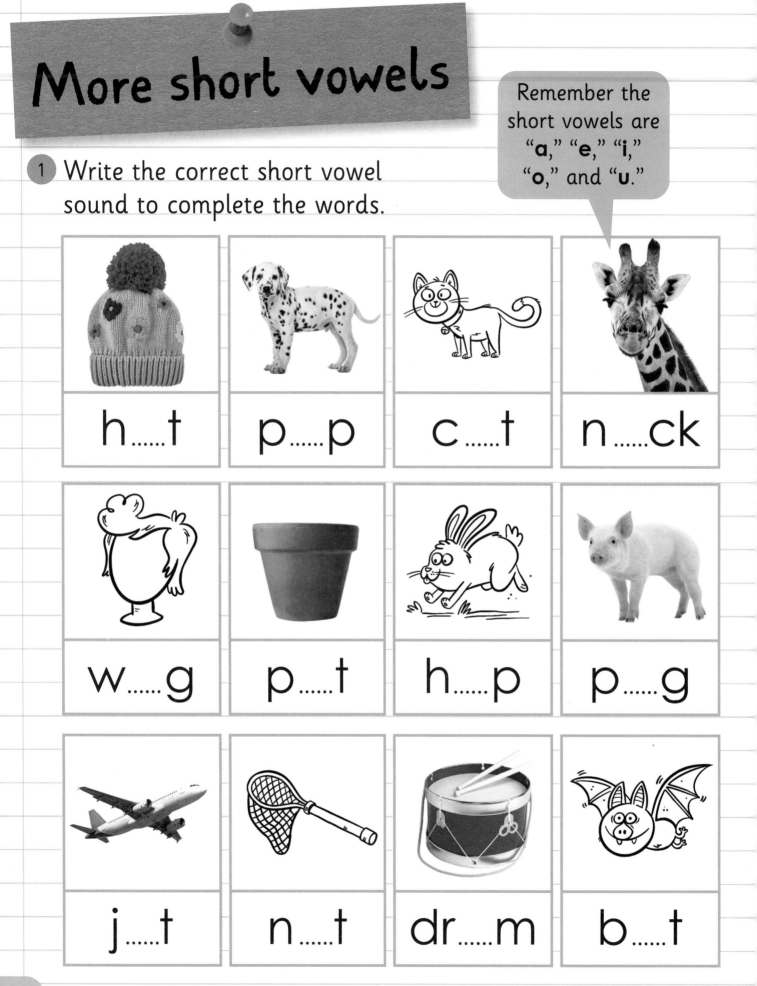

h....t

p....p

c....t

n....ck

w....g

p....t

h....p

p....g

j....t

n....t

dr....m

b....t

Problem and solution

Most stories include a problem and a solution.
A **problem** is something a character wants to fix or figure out. A **solution** is how the problem is fixed or solved.

 Read the text.

> Arzo got a skateboard for his birthday. He stood up on the skateboard but fell down again.
>
> Mom said, "Arzo, let's watch some videos and learn how to ride." Arzo and Mom watched videos and practiced all week.
>
> By the end of the week, Arzo was able to ride his skateboard. "You did it!" Mom cheered.

2 Answer the following questions.

1. What is the problem?

   ....

   ....

2. What is the solution to the problem?

   ....

   ....

Predict

Predict means making a good guess about what will happen.

Good readers make predictions before and while reading a text.

1 Look at the picture on the cover of the book. Predict what the book will be about.

I predict that the book will be about

....

....

2 Look at the pictures from the middle of a different book. Predict what will happen next.

I predict that

....

....

Write the ending

The **ending** of a story usually includes a solution to the problem.

1 Read the text.

The Brown family went on a trip to the beach. It was a long trip, so Dad drove while Mom, Kia, and Kevin went to sleep. Dad drove and drove. After a while, Dad woke up his family. He said, "Oh no! I think we are lost."

2 What happens next?
Write an ending for the story.

Make sure you tell how the Brown family solves their problem.

....
....
....
....
....
....
....
....
....
....

Adjectives

Adjectives are words that describe a person, place, or thing.

1 Circle the adjectives.

(big)	small	green
dinosaur	old	ball
fast	tasty	soft
loud	baby	truck

I am a **big** monster!

2 Choosing from the words below, write the adjective that best describes each dinosaur picture.

spotted   spiky   tiny

....

40

3 Think of an adjective to describe each picture. Write it below.

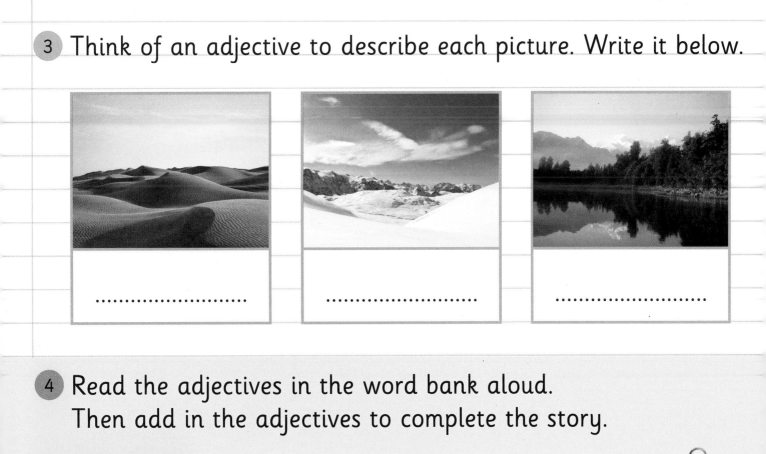

....

4 Read the adjectives in the word bank aloud.
Then add in the adjectives to complete the story.

Word bank
yellow
shiny
~~cold~~
new
blue

It was a ......cold...... night. Mom told Dino
to put on his .... jacket.
"No! I want to wear my .... raincoat,"
said Dino. "I like my .... raincoat
the best." "Okay," said Mom. "Make sure
you wear your .... rain boots, too."

5 Circle the adjective in each sentence.

a. The dinosaur walked across the green grass.
b. That is a beautiful waterfall.
c. Some dinosaurs ate leaves from tall trees.
d. Some dinosaurs had pointy teeth.

41

Shape poems

A **shape poem** is a poem in the shape of an object. The words and phrases used in the poem usually describe that object.

1 Read the shape poem about pizza.

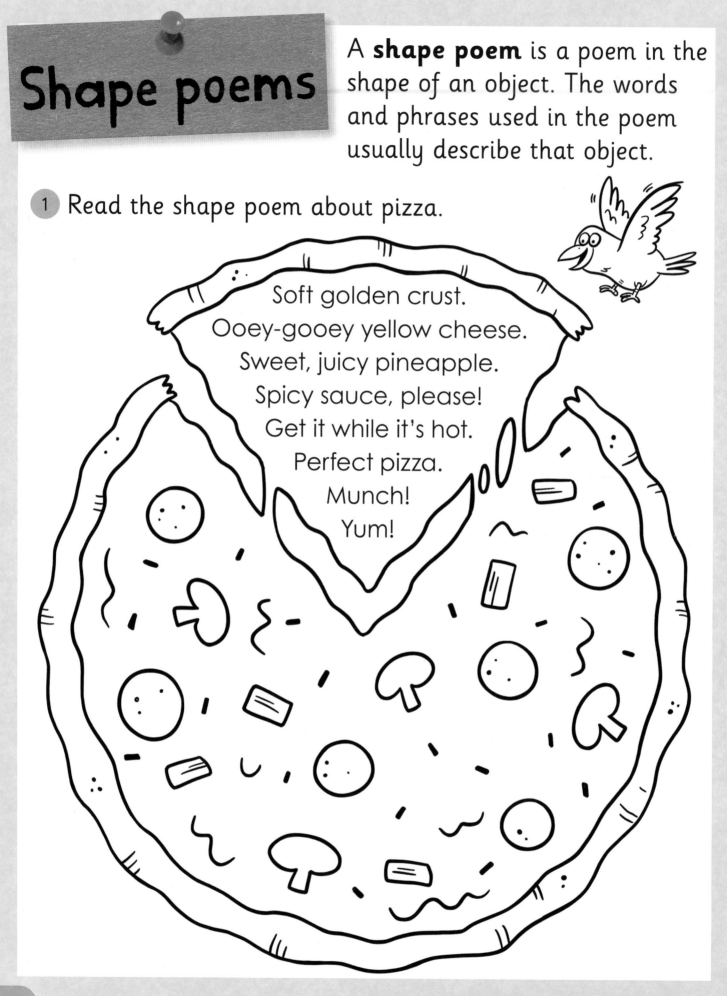

Soft golden crust.
Ooey-gooey yellow cheese.
Sweet, juicy pineapple.
Spicy sauce, please!
Get it while it's hot.
Perfect pizza.
Munch!
Yum!

2 Which words from the pizza poem relate to the five senses? Write them below.

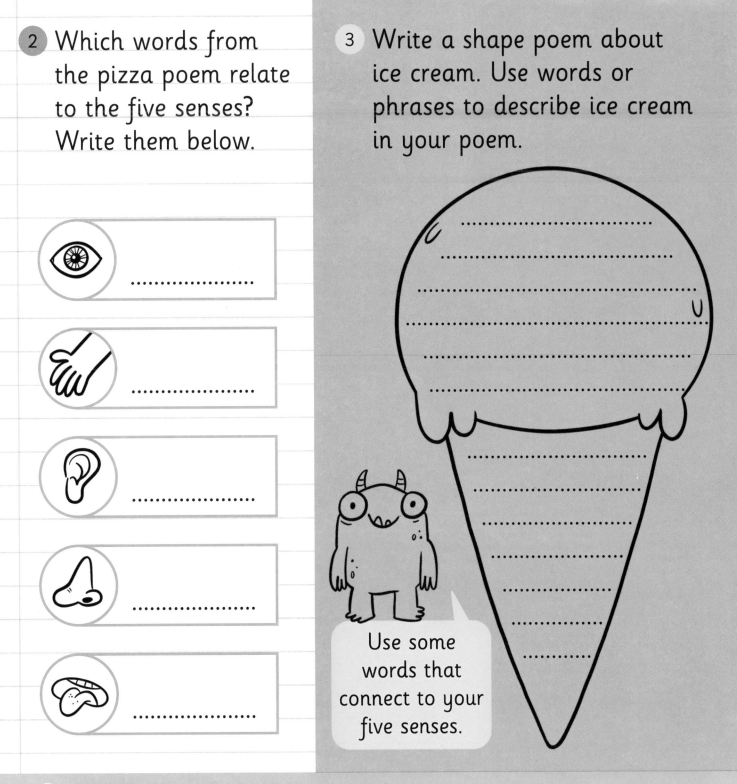

3 Write a shape poem about ice cream. Use words or phrases to describe ice cream in your poem.

Use some words that connect to your five senses.

4 Which words in your ice cream poem connect to the five senses? Write them below.

Sight	Touch	Sound	Smell	Taste
....	....	....	....	....

Beginning blends

Blends are two or three letters that keep their own sounds when put together.

Blends can be at the **beginning** of a word.

1 Color in the correct beginning blend for each picture.

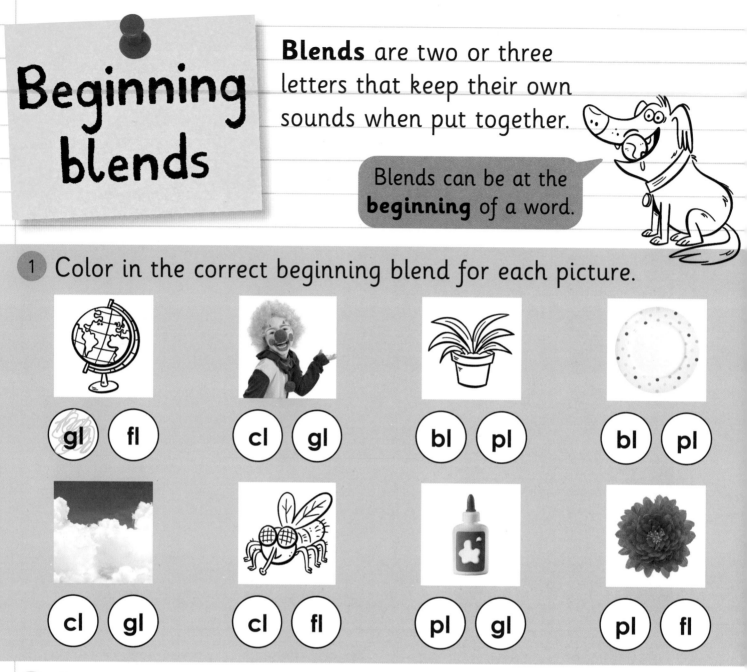

gl / fl	cl / gl	bl / pl	bl / pl
cl / gl	cl / fl	pl / gl	pl / fl

2 Can you match each of these words to an example?

| plus | gloves | black | climb |

Something to keep your hands warm	+	Go up using your hands and feet	
.......gloves.......	....	....	....

44

3 Choose the correct "**br**" or "**pr**" blend for each word.

..........oom   ....esent   ....ice

..........ead   ....ush   ....ize

4 Choose the correct "**gr**" or "**cr**" blend for each word.

..........ab   ....ane   ....een

..........apes   ....ow   ....in

More beginning blends

1 Fill in the correct blend to complete the words.

sc	sn	~~sp~~	sw

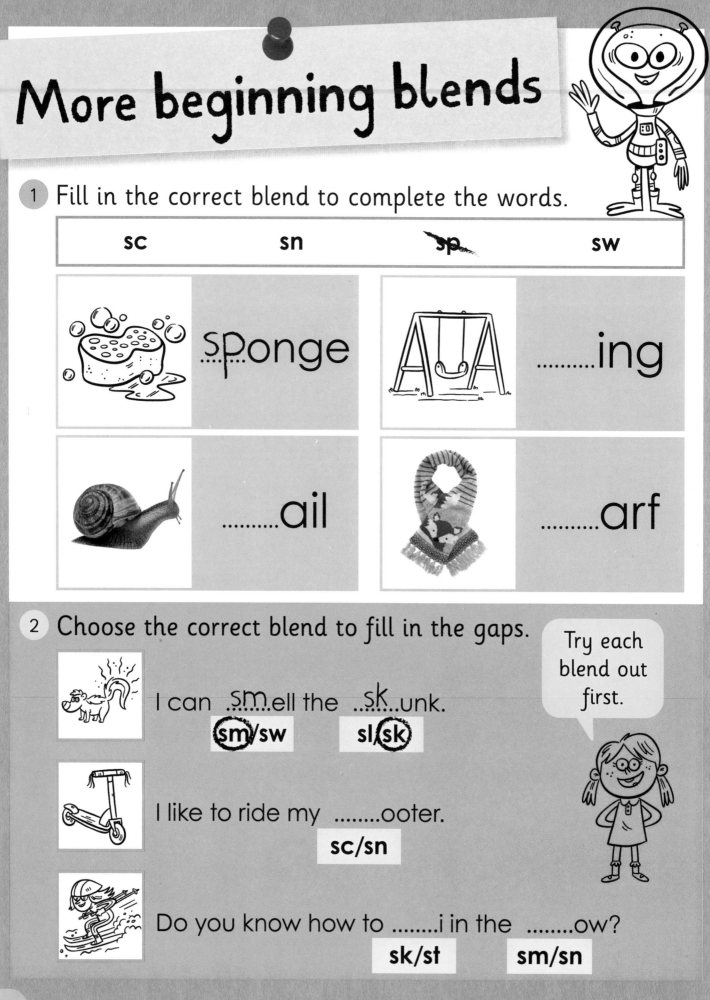

sponge

.........ing

.........ail

.........arf

2 Choose the correct blend to fill in the gaps.

I can ..sm..ell the ..sk..unk.

(sm)/sw   sl/(sk)

Try each blend out first.

I like to ride my ....ooter.

sc/sn

Do you know how to ....i in the ....ow?

sk/st   sm/sn

Retell

Retell means to tell the important parts of the story, including characters, setting, beginning, middle, and end.

1 Read the text.

Jo and Akim went to the park to play soccer.
Akim brought his ball. They started to play.
Jo took a shot at the goal. She kicked the ball hard.
Oh no! The ball shot over the fence and into a
yard. Akim ran to the fence. A man was in the
yard. He picked up the ball and gave it to Akim.
"Thank you," said Akim. Jo and Akim started to play again.

2 Who are the characters?

1. ....
2. ....
3. ....

3 Where is the setting?

....
....

4 Write what happened at the beginning, in the middle, and at the end of the story.

Beginning	Middle	End
....	....	....
....	....	....
....	....	....
....	....	....
....	....	....

The **main topic** describes what the text is mostly about.

1 Read the text.

Plants have many parts. Each plant part has a special job.
Roots hold the plant in the ground. They help plants
get water and food to live.
The **stem** holds the plant up. It also helps carry
water and food through the plant.
The **leaves** use water, air, and sunlight to make food.
The **flowers** bring insects that help the plant grow seeds.
The **seeds** can grow into new plants.

2 What is the main topic of the text? Circle the correct answer.

a. Animal parts

b. Plant parts

c. Body parts

Check the text for your answer.

3 Use the bold words from the text to help label the parts of a plant.

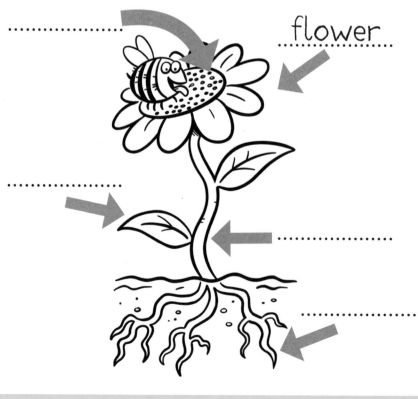

flower

Sort words

Words can be sorted into **groups** or categories to show a connection.

1 Write each word in the correct group.

piano	doll	violin	robot
drum	ball	flute	teddy bear

Toys	Instruments

2 Read the words in each category.
Write a name to describe each category.

....

red	yellow	kiwi	mango
green	pink	watermelon	pear

3 Write four words for the category "**clothes**."

....

....

49

Sight words

Sight words are common words found in text. They should be recognized quickly by sight.

① Read and trace each sight word.
Then write each word in two colors.

Read the word	Trace the word	Write the word in two different colors
of	of	of of
give	give	
put	put	
were	were	

② Find each of the sight words in the word search.

Sight words are also called high-frequency words or tricky words.

p	w	e	r	e	g
x	v	o	p	w	i
m	p	u	t	g	v
g	y	v	o	f	e

☐ of
☐ give
☐ put
☐ were

More sight words

1 Read and trace each sight word.
Then write each word in two colors.

Read the word	Trace the word	Write the word in two different colors
her	her	
walk	walk	
again	again	
know	know	

2 Circle the correct letters to spell each sight word.

her	m (h) i a (e) (r) f s
walk	w i a c l k c
again	a j g a l i n m
know	l k t n o u w x

Nouns

A **noun** is a person, animal, place, or thing.

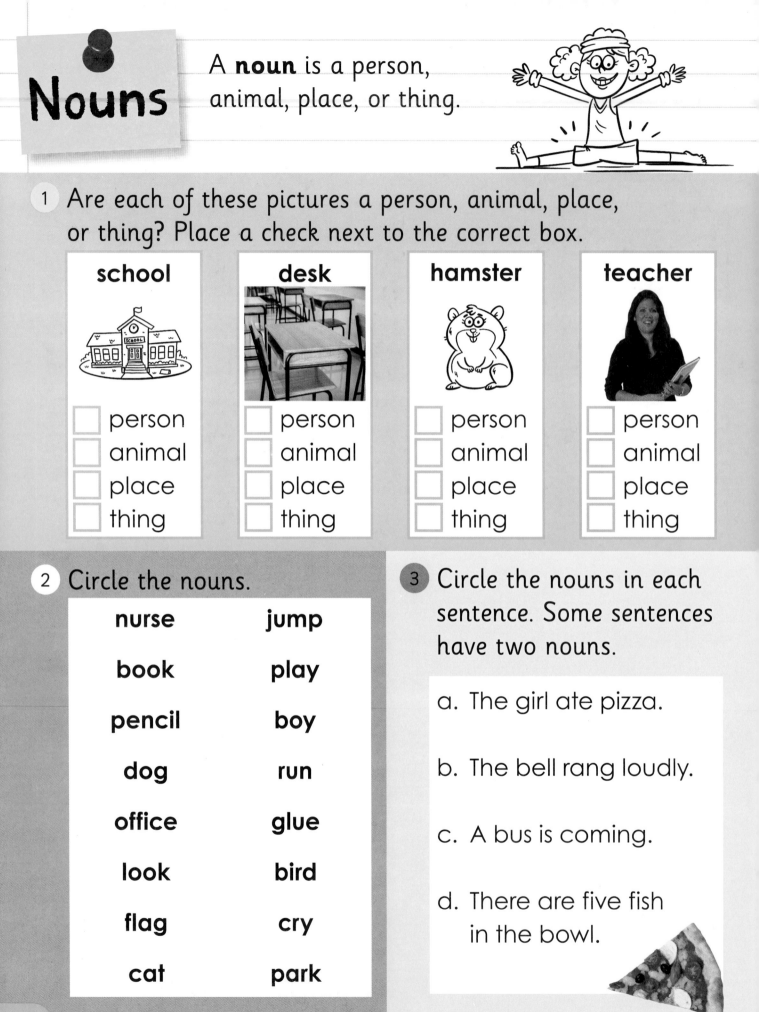

1. Are each of these pictures a person, animal, place, or thing? Place a check next to the correct box.

school

☐ person
☐ animal
☐ place
☐ thing

desk

☐ person
☐ animal
☐ place
☐ thing

hamster

☐ person
☐ animal
☐ place
☐ thing

teacher

☐ person
☐ animal
☐ place
☐ thing

2. Circle the nouns.

nurse	jump
book	play
pencil	boy
dog	run
office	glue
look	bird
flag	cry
cat	park

3. Circle the nouns in each sentence. Some sentences have two nouns.

a. The girl ate pizza.

b. The bell rang loudly.

c. A bus is coming.

d. There are five fish in the bowl.

Proper nouns

A **proper noun** names a specific person, place, or thing.

For example, New York is a proper noun. It is the name of a city.

Proper nouns need a capital letter.

1 Circle all the proper nouns.

city	Mrs. Jones	Scotland	chocolate
woman	Europe	rat	Hannah

2 Fill in the chart by writing a proper noun next to each common noun.

Common noun	Proper noun
month	October
boy	
country	
planet	
city	

Word bank

October
Mars
Jack
Boston
Canada

3 Write your name, the town, and the country where you live. Remember to use a capital letter at the beginning of each word.

1. ....

2. ....

3. ....

Possessive nouns

A **possessive noun** shows ownership of a person, place, or thing. To show ownership, add an apostrophe ' and the letter "**s**." For example, "Kim**'s** bike" shows a possessive noun.

1 Choose a noun from the word bank to finish each sentence. Add **'s** to make the noun possessive.

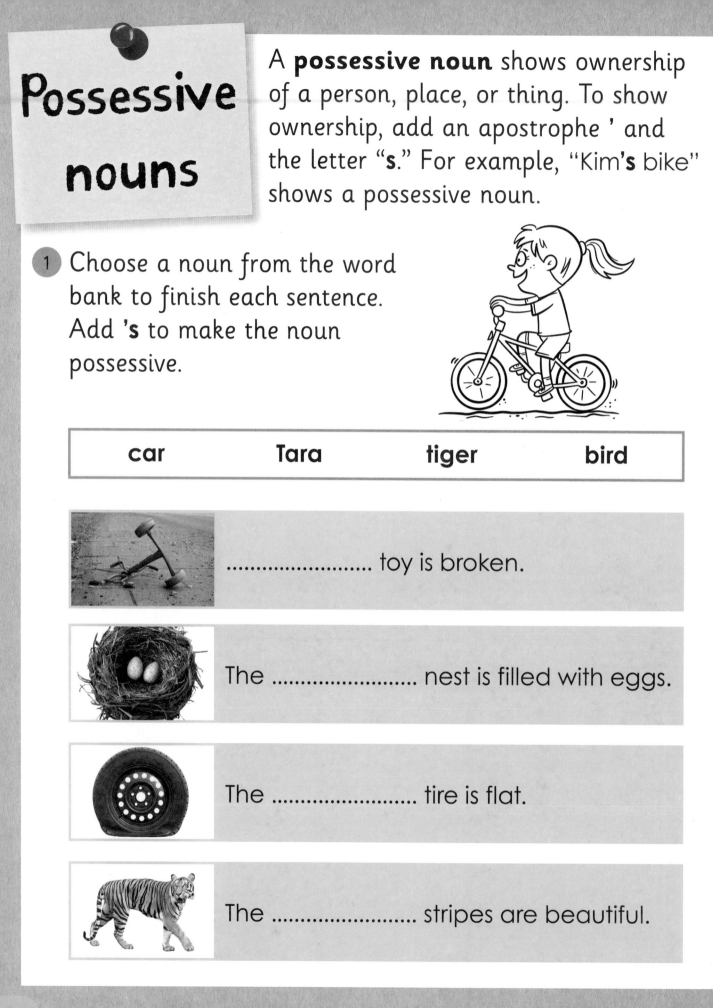

| car | Tara | tiger | bird |

.... toy is broken.

The .... nest is filled with eggs.

The .... tire is flat.

The .... stripes are beautiful.

Making connections

Making connections means learning how things are related. Readers can make connections between people, events, and information in a text.

1 Read the text.

> **Turtles and tortoises**
>
> Many people think a turtle and a tortoise are the same.
> They are both reptiles with shells, but they are not the same.
> A turtle lives in the water. A tortoise lives on land.
> They both lay their eggs on land.
> A turtle has a light flat shell. A tortoise has a heavy round shell.
> They have different feet, too. A turtle has webbed feet to
> help it swim. A tortoise has short, chubby feet to help it walk.
> Can you tell the difference between a turtle and a tortoise?

2 Make a connection.
Tell two ways that a turtle and a tortoise are the **same**.
1. ....
2. ....

3 Make a connection.
Tell two ways that a turtle and a tortoise are **different**.
1. ....
2. ....

Final blends

Blends are two or three letters that keep their individual sounds when together. Blends can also be found at the end of a word.

These are also called **final blends**.

1 Add the final blend to make each word. Write the word, then draw a picture.

	ld		
Add the blend	chi.**ld**.	co.......	go.......
Add the word	child	....	....
Draw a picture			

	lt		
Add the blend	me.......	be.......	qui.......
Add the word	....	....	....
Draw a picture			

2 Choose the correct blend for each word.

nk	mp	lk

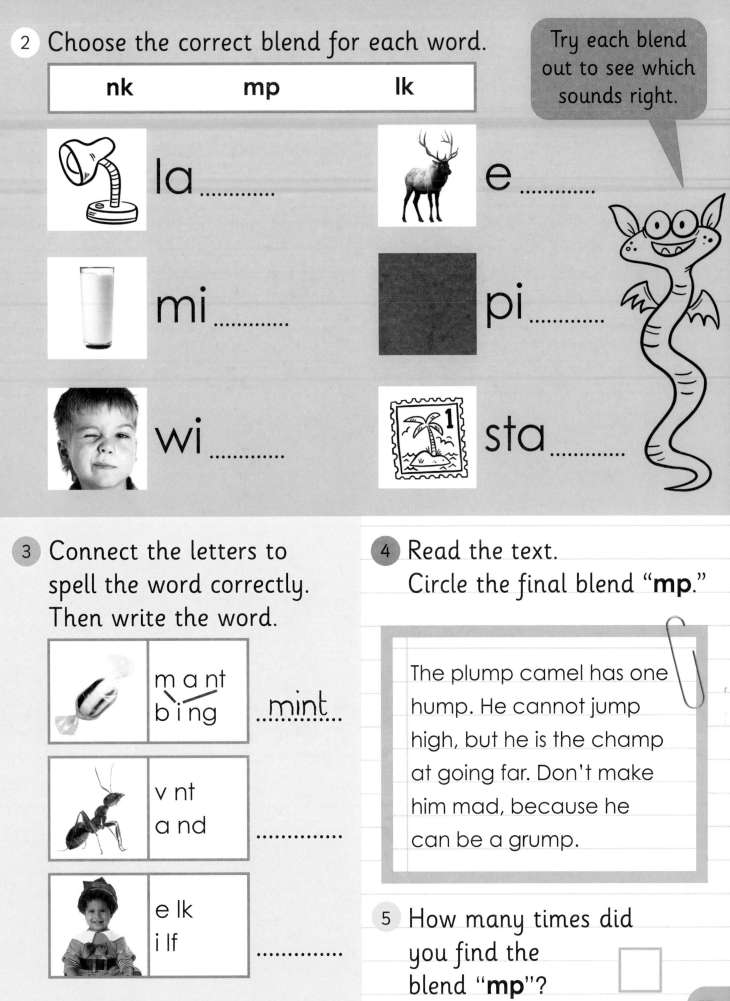

la............

e............

mi............

pi............

wi............

sta............

Try each blend out to see which sounds right.

3 Connect the letters to spell the word correctly. Then write the word.

m a nt
b i ng   ..mint..

v nt
a nd   ....

e lk
i lf   ....

4 Read the text. Circle the final blend "**mp**."

The plump camel has one hump. He cannot jump high, but he is the champ at going far. Don't make him mad, because he can be a grump.

5 How many times did you find the blend "**mp**"?

57

Fairy tales

A **fairy tale** is a fiction story with magic. Some well-known fairy tales are "Snow White," "Jack and the Beanstalk," and "Goldilocks and the Three Bears."

1 What is your favorite fairy tale?

....

2 A fairy tale has special details. Write the special details for your favorite fairy tale in the boxes below.

Good characters	Evil characters	Magic
....	....	....
....	....	....
....	....	....
....	....	....
....	....	....
....	....	....
....	....	....
....	....	....
....	....	....
....	....	....

3 Does your favorite fairy tale have a happy ending?

....

Multiple-meaning words

Multiple-meaning words are words that have the same spelling and same pronunciation but have different meanings.

"**Bark**" is a word that has different meanings. It can mean the sound a dog makes or a part of a tree.

1 Check the picture that shows the correct meaning of the word in bold.

I mailed a **letter**.

The **mouse** ran across the room.

Oh no! The **fly** landed on my food.

2 Read the sentences.
Circle the correct meaning for the word in bold.

a. Every Saturday morning, I like to **bowl**.

   a dish for food   play a game with a rolling ball

b. Does wood **sink** or float in water?

   go to the bottom   a place to wash your hands

Personal pronouns

A **personal pronoun** is a word that takes the place of a noun.

Some personal pronouns are: **I**, **he**, **she**, **you**, **it**, **we**, **they**, **me**, **him**, **her**, **them**, and **us**.

1 Circle the personal pronoun in each sentence.

    a. Help me!

    b. How are you?

    c. We like to bake cakes.

    d. The bus driver took them to school.

2 Write the correct personal pronoun for each sentence.

    a. .... ate the candy.
       She/Her

Only one word will make sense in each sentence.

    b. .... baked cookies.
       He/Him

    c. Come play with .... !
            us/we

    d. .... went to the candy store.
      Them/They

    e. Give it to ....
        I/me

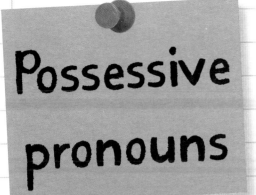

Possessive pronouns

Some **pronouns** tell us who owns something or whose turn it is. **Mine, yours, ours, his, hers,** and **theirs** tells us about who owns something or whose turn it might be.

1 Choose a word to complete each sentence.

~~yours~~	mine	theirs	ours	hers

a. This is your ball. The ball is ....yours........ .

b. The hat belongs to me. The hat is ....

c. John and Ellen live in that house. The house is ....

d. The girl has a red purse. The purse is ....

e. My family has a black car. The car is ....

2 Circle the correct pronoun for each sentence.

The vanilla milkshake is hers/ours.

The blue camera is his/yours.

Question words

Question words are used to ask a question. **Who, what, when, where, why,** and **how** are question words.

1 Circle the question words in each sentence.

a. (How) do you play the guitar?

b. When does school start?

c. What did you eat for lunch?

d. Who did that?

e. Where is my dog?

2 Write the correct question word to complete each sentence.

a. .... do you live?

b. .... many days are there until Halloween?

c. .... do you go to bed?

d. .... is your best friend?

e. .... instrument do you play?

Word bank

Who
What
When
Where
How

3 Turn each sentence into a question.

Remember that questions end with a question mark.

a. Layla plays basketball.

Where does Layla play basketball?

b. The rocket is very fast.

....

c. Reagan is feeling sad.

....

d. My next music concert is in May.

....

4 Write a question for each picture.

....

.............................? ....?

Ask and answer questions

Key details are important pieces of information in a text. Readers use key details to **ask and answer questions**.

1 Read the text.

Bats are amazing mammals! Did you know that bats are the only mammals that can fly?
They have the best hearing of all land mammals.
Bats make sounds that bounce back to their huge ears. This is how they find insects to eat.
Bats do most of their hunting at night.
They are nocturnal. This means they are awake at night.
During the day, bats sleep hanging upside down with a big group of other bats.

2 Answer these questions.
1. What do bats like to eat? ....
2. What do bats do during the day? ....

....

3 Check all the sentences that are true.

☐ Bats stay awake at night.

☐ Bats can hear very well.

☐ Bats can't fly.

4 What else do you want to know about bats? Write one question that you have.

....

....

....?

Articles

Articles are special words that come before a noun. The words "**a**," "**an**," and "**the**" are articles.

Remember, a noun is a person, place, or thing.

"**a**" is used before a word that starts with a **consonant**.

"**an**" is used before a word that starts with a **vowel**: "**a**," "**e**," "**i**," "**o**," or "**u**."

1 Write the correct article "**a**" or "**an**" before each noun.

...... motorcycle   ...... bus   ...... airplane

...... ambulance   ...... train   ...... submarine

2 Write the correct article for each sentence.

| a | an | the |

"**the**" is used before a specific noun.

a. .... fastest train goes 373 miles per hour!
b. .... submarine can stay underwater for many months.
c. .... ambulance has special equipment to help sick people.
d. The wind can change the speed of .... hot-air balloon.

Digraphs

Digraphs are two letters that make one sound when they are together.

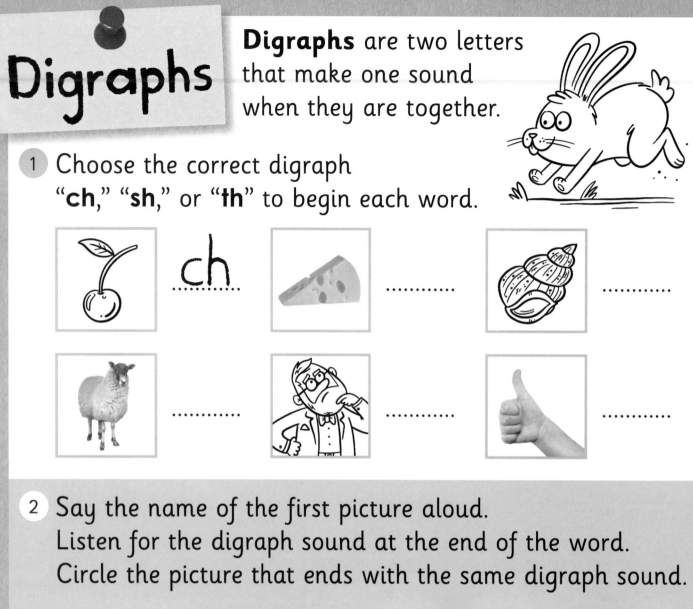

1 Choose the correct digraph "**ch**," "**sh**," or "**th**" to begin each word.

ch ....

....

2 Say the name of the first picture aloud.
Listen for the digraph sound at the end of the word.
Circle the picture that ends with the same digraph sound.

bath | teeth | hat

lunch | sock | beach

push | house | fish

3 "**Wh**" and "**wr**" are digraphs. Write the correct digraph to complete each word.

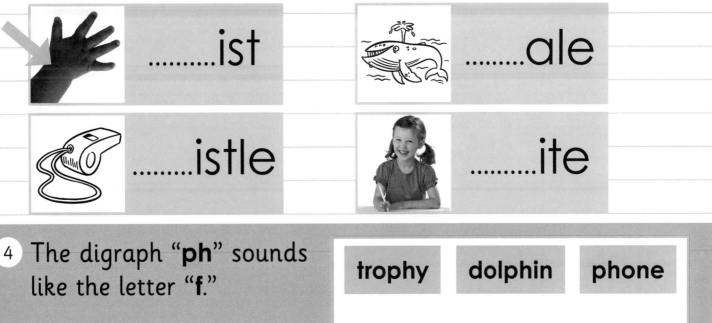

..........ist

.........ale

.........istle

..........ite

4 The digraph "**ph**" sounds like the letter "**f**."

Read each word and then draw a line to match it to the correct picture.

trophy   dolphin   phone

5 The digraph "**kn**" sounds like the letter "**n**."
Read the words with the digraph "**kn**" aloud.
Choose the correct word to complete each sentence.

a. You need a fork and .... to cut the pancakes.

b. I have a big .... in my shoelaces.

c. Jessie hurt her .... playing soccer.

d. The .... was riding a horse.

Word bank

knot

knight

knife

knee

Verbs

A **verb** is an action word. It names something you can do.

> **Sing, dance,** and **play** are all verbs.

1 Read the verbs aloud. Then write the correct verb next to each picture.

drink	eat	~~ride~~	run	climb

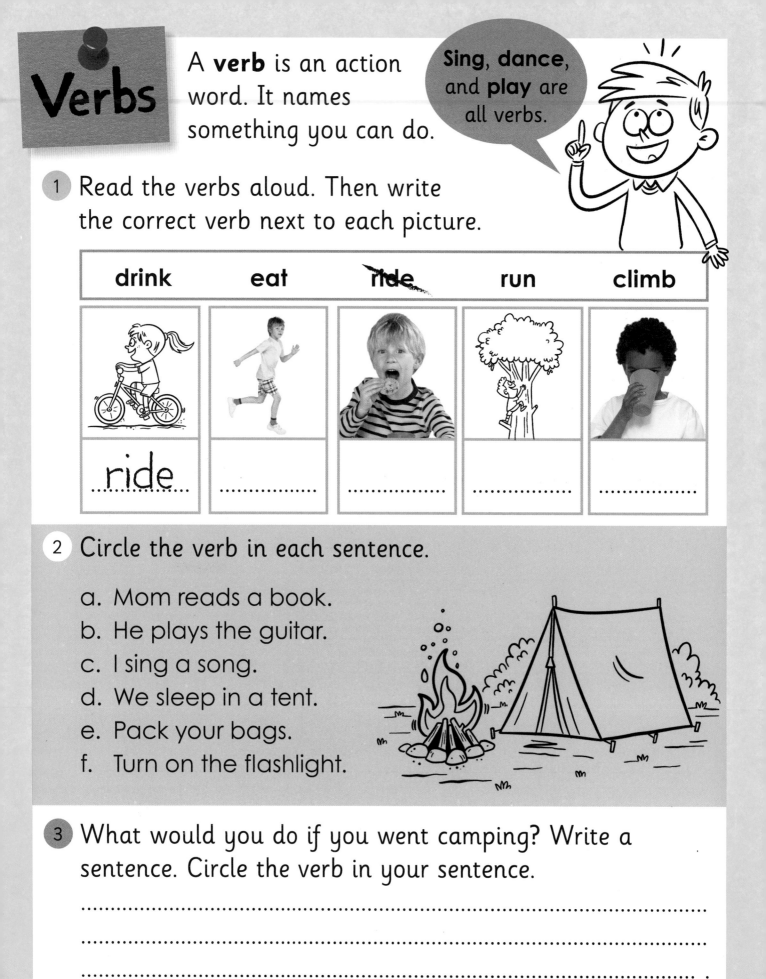

ride ....

2 Circle the verb in each sentence.

a. Mom reads a book.
b. He plays the guitar.
c. I sing a song.
d. We sleep in a tent.
e. Pack your bags.
f. Turn on the flashlight.

3 What would you do if you went camping? Write a sentence. Circle the verb in your sentence.

....

....

....

Verb tenses

A **verb** in the **present tense** names an action that is happening **now**.

A **verb** in the **past tense** names an action that has **already happened**.

1 Complete the chart with present tense and past tense verbs.

Some past tense verbs end with the letters "**ed**."

Present tense	Past tense
cook	cooked
play	
	jumped
	helped
dance	
shout	

2 Underline the past tense verbs in each sentence.

a. We walked in the garden.
b. We planted two trees yesterday.
c. They picked some flowers.
d. The dogs barked and jumped.
e. The cat chased a bee.
f. We looked at the stars in the sky.

Shades of meaning

Some words have similar meanings. Although some words have similar meanings, there are small differences between them. This is called **shades of meaning**.

1 Read the word. Then write a word with a similar meaning.

little .....tiny........   jump ....   cry ....

big ....   cute ....   hug ....

2 Read the three words in each set.
Put them in order from weakest to strongest.

furious, mad, angry	....	....	....
warm, burning, hot	....	....	....

3 Read the words in the chart. Choose two words with similar meanings. Put them in order from weakest to strongest.

~~gulp~~	happy	~~drink~~
excited	sprint	jog

	Weakest	·········▶ Strongest
sip	drink	gulp
glad		
walk		

Final "e"

When "**e**" is the final letter in a word, it is usually silent. The other vowel in the word makes its long vowel sound.

Shh!

① Read the word in the first column. Then make a new word by adding a final "**e**."

② Mix the letters to make a word with a final "**e**."

not.......

cap.......

cub.......

bit.......

tub......

m l e i
....

a e p t
....

t e n u
....

e r s o
....

How to

"**How to**" writing describes the steps needed to do something.

Always ask an adult to help with the blender.

1 Read the smoothie recipe.

How to make a strawberry smoothie

You will need:
2 cups of strawberries
1 banana
1 cup of ice
1/2 cup of water
A blender

Steps:
1. Put the strawberries in the blender.
2. Add the banana.
3. Add the ice to the blender.
4. Pour water over the strawberries, banana, and ice.
5. Put the lid on the blender tightly.
6. Turn the blender on high.
7. Blend for one minute or until smooth.

2 Put these steps in order using the numbers 1, 2, or 3.

☐ Add the banana.

☐ Blend for one minute.

☐ Add ice to the blender.

3 Which is not an ingredient to make a strawberry smoothie? Cross it out.

strawberries
milk
banana
ice

4 Think of the many things that you know how to do.
Write one thing that you could explain to someone.

I can explain how to ....

....

....

....

....

....

5 Write a list of the things you will need to brush your teeth:

You will need:

1. ....

2. ....

3. ....

4. ....

6 Write a list of the steps in order to brush your teeth.

Method:

1. ....

2. ....

3. ....

Long vowel "a"

The long "a" sound can be made using "**ay**" or "**ai**."

1 Read each word aloud.
Then write each word in the correct egg basket.

hay	lay	rain	ray
play	tail	wait	paid

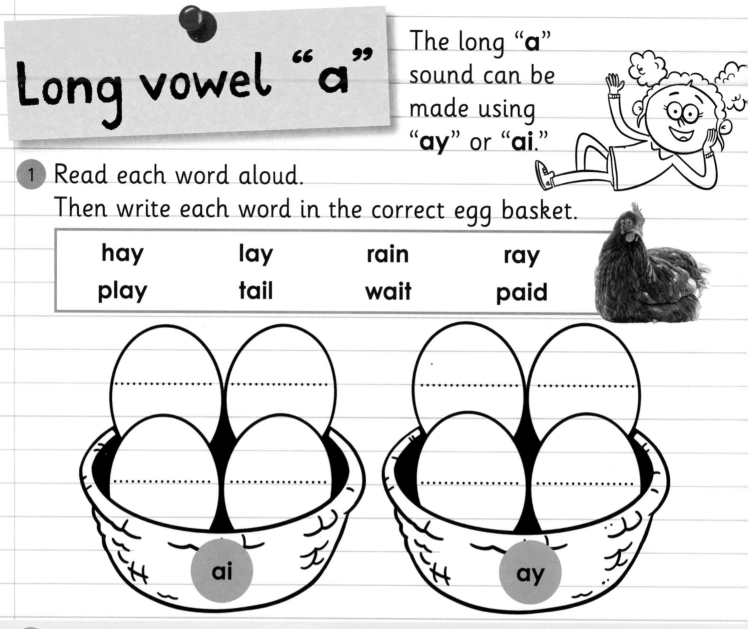

ai

ay

2 Read the "**ai**" and "**ay**" words aloud. Find each word in the word search.

☐ nail
☐ away
☐ rainbow
☐ day

r	a	i	n	b	o	w
c	y	k	v	i	e	l
n	j	q	h	r	t	a
a	w	f	p	i	e	w
i	u	d	a	y	o	a
l	g	m	s	x	d	y

Long vowel "e"

The long "e" sound can be made using "ee," "ea," or "ey."

When two vowels work together, it is called a **vowel pattern** or a **vowel team**.

1 Color the candy with the "**ee**" pattern red.
Color the candy with the "**ea**" pattern yellow.
Color the candy with the "**ey**" pattern green.

keep   each   peas   seed   eat

honey   cheek   peach   donkey   clean

2 Read the words aloud. Add them to the story below.

| teeth | treat | green | beans | sweets |

I went to the candy store to get a ....
My mom said too many .... could hurt
my ....
I got some jelly ....
I like the .... jelly beans the best.

Long vowel "i"

The long "i" sound can be made using "**igh**," "**ie**," or "**i-e**."

1 Read the words with the long "i" vowel pattern.

tie	sigh	size	night	cried

hide	fight	fries	prize

2 Write each of the words from Activity 1 under the correct vowel pattern.

p**ie**

1. ....

2. ....

3. ....

Read the example word first to check which long "i" sound it is.

l**igh**t

1. ....

2. ....

3. ....

k**i**t**e**

1. ....

2. ....

3. ....

Long vowel "o"

The long "o" sound can be made using "oa," "oe," or "o-e."

1 Follow the words in the maze with a long "o" vowel pattern to help the goat get to the toad.

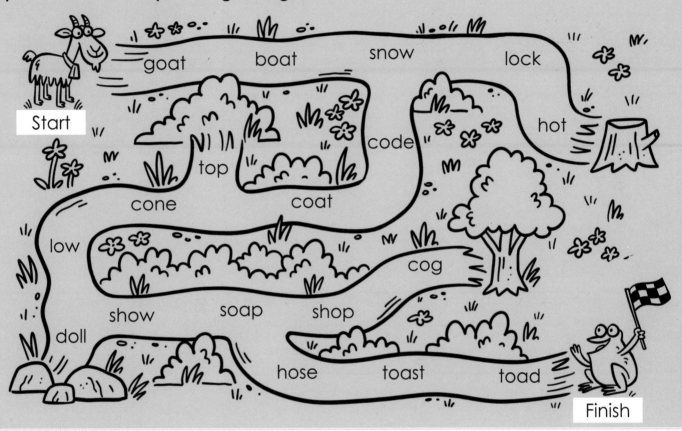

Start

goat   boat   snow   lock

code   hot

top

cone   coat

low

cog

show   soap   shop

doll

hose   toast   toad

Finish

2 Color the words with the "ow" vowel pattern blue.
Color the words with the "oa" vowel pattern green.
Color the words with the "o-e" vowel pattern orange.

soap   mow   coach   rose

road

own   row

bone

Long vowel "u"

The long "u" sound can be made using "ew," "ue," or "ui."

1 Check each of the words with the correct long "u" spelling.

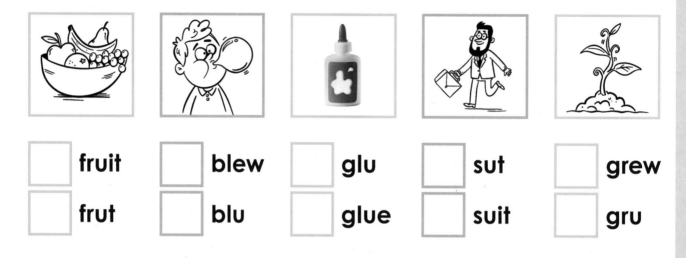

☐ fruit	☐ blew	☐ glu	☐ sut	☐ grew
☐ frut	☐ blu	☐ glue	☐ suit	☐ gru

2 Read the words aloud.
Write the correct word next to each definition.

> **chew**   **clue**   **cruise**

a. A trip on a large boat. ....

b. To make food smaller using your teeth. ....

c. A hint that helps solve the problem. ....

3 Read the sentences. Circle all the words with a long "u" vowel pattern.

> Each sentence has more than one!

a. The blue plane flew over the ocean.

b. I have a few books due to the library.

c. I wish I knew how to make stew.

Check back to pages 74 to 78 if you need help.

1 Spell the word using the correct final "e" vowel pattern.

a-e	o-e	i-e	u-e

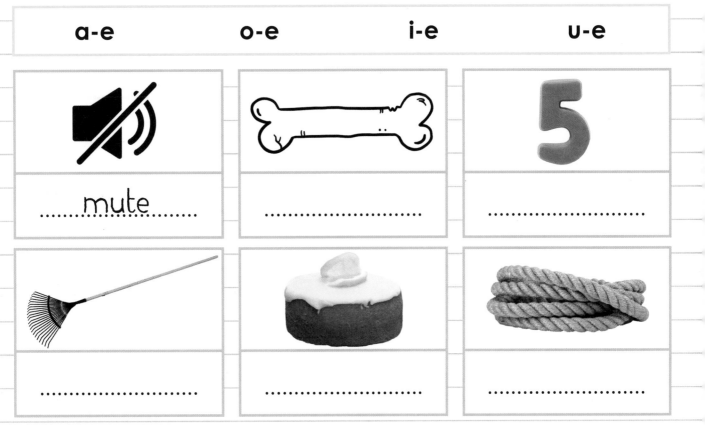

mute

2 Read the words aloud and listen for a long vowel sound. Cross out the word in each row that does not have a long vowel sound.

Long "a"	are	wait	cave	day
Long "e"	need	mean	Pete	rest
Long "i"	lip	time	high	lie
Long "o"	know	vote	lock	loaf
Long "u"	juice	chew	use	cut

Temporal words

Temporal words describe the order of events in a story. Some examples of temporal words are **first**, **next**, **then**, **last**, and **finally**. Temporal words are also called transition words.

1 Draw a line from each temporal word to the part of a story where it would be used.

first		finally
last	beginning	next
then	middle	at the end
in the beginning	end	once upon a time

2 Fill in numbers 1, 2, or 3 to put the story of Drake Dragon in order.

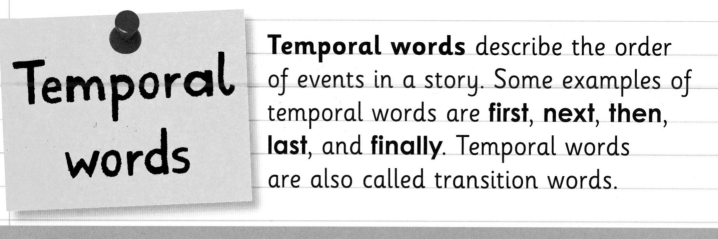

[ ] **Then** Drake asked his mom for help.
[ ] **After** his mom helped him, Drake could fly.
[ ] The **first** time Drake tried to fly, he fell to the ground.

3 Fill in numbers 1, 2, 3, or 4 to put the story of Uma Unicorn in order.

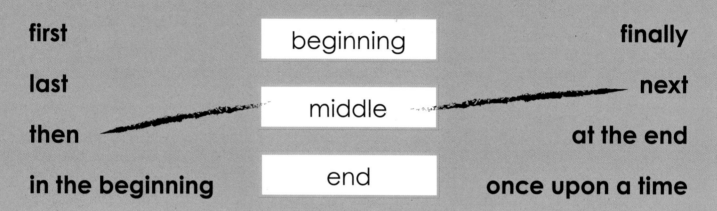

[ ] **Finally**, Uma ate dinner and went to sleep.
[ ] **After** playing for a long time, Uma went home.
[ ] **Next**, she saw her friends and played with them.
[ ] **One day**, Uma Unicorn went for a walk in the forest.

Using temporal words

Writers use **temporal words** to share their ideas in order.

Think about your favorite day.

1 **What are three things that happened that day?**

My favorite day was my birthday party!

1. ....

2. ....

3. ....

2 Write a story about your day using temporal words for the beginning, middle, and end of the story.

Syllables

"**Apple**" has two syllables. Clap twice as you say the word.

Words can be broken into parts called **syllables**. You can clap to count the syllables in a word.

1 Read each word aloud. Clap the number of syllables.

1 syllable		2 syllables		3 syllables	
owl	bat	penguin	turtle	crocodile	koala

2 Read each word aloud and clap the number of syllables. Circle the correct number of syllables for each word.

cat	lion	fox	gorilla	duck
①2 3	1 2 3	1 2 3	1 2 3	1 2 3

rabbit	giraffe	fly	parrot
1 2 3	1 2 3	1 2 3	1 2 3

(3) Read each word aloud. Clap for each syllable.
Write the word in the correct column.

| map | camel | deer | zookeeper |
| monkey | elephant | bear | panda |

1 syllable	**2 syllables**	**3 syllables**
1.	1.	1. ....
2.	2.	2. ....
3.	3.	

Words with one syllable do not need to be broken into parts.

(4) Clap then write the number of syllables in each word. Following the example, draw a line to break the written words into syllables.

	Number of syllables	**Show syllables**
	2	ti/g e r
	....	s l o t h
	....	f l a m i n g o

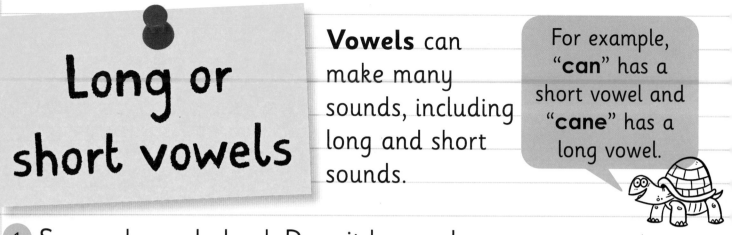

Long or short vowels

Vowels can make many sounds, including long and short sounds.

For example, "**can**" has a short vowel and "**cane**" has a long vowel.

1. Say each word aloud. Does it have a long or short vowel sound? Circle the correct answer.

June	plan	show	meat	end
(long) short	long short	long short	long short	long short

tray	slime	duck	trim	blob
long short	long short	long short	long short	long short

2. Color the words with a long vowel sound yellow. Color the words with a short vowel sound blue.

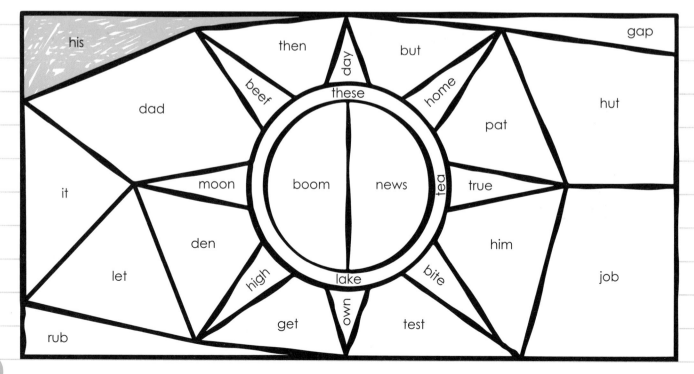

his · then · day · but · gap · beef · these · home · hut · dad · pat · moon · boom · news · tea · true · it · den · him · let · high · lake · bite · job · rub · get · own · test

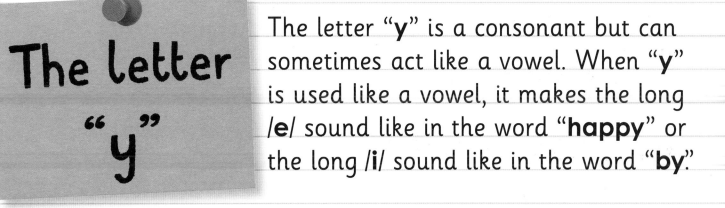

The letter "y"

The letter "**y**" is a consonant but can sometimes act like a vowel. When "**y**" is used like a vowel, it makes the long /**e**/ sound like in the word "**happy**" or the long /**i**/ sound like in the word "**by**."

1 If the letter "**y**" sounds like long /**e**/ color the leaf green.
If the letter "**y**" sounds like long /**i**/ color the leaf red.
If the letter "**y**" sounds like consonant /**y**/ color the leaf orange.

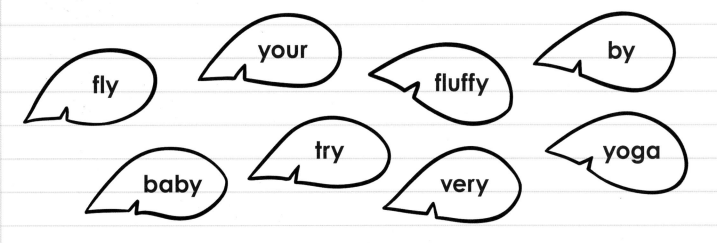

fly   your   fluffy   by   try   baby   very   yoga

2 Sort each word into the correct group.

sky	yes	lucky	tiny	cry	yet

Sounds like long "e"	Sounds like long "i"	Sounds like consonant "y"
....	....	....
....	....	....

Singular and plural nouns

Singular means one person, place, or thing.

Plural means more than one person, place, or thing.

1 Color the words that describe one thing red.
Color the words that describe more than one thing blue.

 moons sun 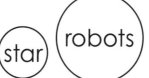 planets star robots alien

2 Many nouns can be made plural by adding an "**s**" to the end of the word. Make the nouns plural by adding "**s**."

Singular	Plural
satellite	satellites
bed	....
rocket	....
helmet	....
girl	....

3 Some nouns are made plural by adding "**es**" to the end of the word. Make the nouns plural by adding "**es**."

Singular	Plural
dish	dishes
bench	....
glass	....
box	....
brush	....

Nouns that end in "**ch**," "**sh**," "**s**," or "**z**" need an "**es**" at the end.

Nouns and verbs

When a noun is **plural**, the verb that comes after it does not end in "**s**."

When a noun is **singular**, the verb that comes after it ends in "**s**."

1 Circle the correct verb for each sentence.

a. The monsters (eat/eats) chips.

For example:
The **ball rolls** down the hill.

b. A troll (live/lives) under the bridge.

c. Dragons (stay/stays) near the castle.

d. The witch (make/makes) a potion.

e. A toad (sing/sings) a song.

f. Mermaids (swim/swims) in the ocean.

2 Write a sentence about a friendly monster who has a soccer ball. Choose the correct verb to use in your sentence.

play	plays

Is the noun singular or plural?

....

....

....

Context clues

1 Use the other words in the sentence to figure out the meaning of the bold word. Circle the correct meaning.

a. She is feeling **drowsy** because she stayed up late.

sleepy or **happy**

b. After lunch, the children quickly **dash** to recess.

run or **wait**

c. I walked **briskly** to catch up to my sister.

quickly or **slowly**

2 Read the sentence and look at the picture. Use the context clues to determine the meaning of the word in bold. Write the meaning of the word below.

Joseph was so cold that his body started to **shiver**.

Use the picture to help!

Shiver means ....

88

3 Read the text.

Mommy Squirrel had a problem, so she asked Ruby Rabbit for help. She told Ruby that Little Squirrel was **missing**. "When was the last time you saw him?" Ruby asked.

"I saw him this morning. We were looking for nuts. Then I **hurried** home, but he stayed out to play," Mommy Squirrel said.

Ruby went to find out more. She looked until she found Little Squirrel's paw prints. Oh no! Little Squirrel was stuck in the mud. Ruby pulled him out and took him home to Mommy Squirrel. "Thank you!" Mommy Squirrel said.

Little Squirrel and Mommy Squirrel were **delighted** to be together again.

4 Use the text above to answer the questions.

Find each difficult word in the story and reread the sentence. Swap the word with your answer to see if it makes sense.

1. What does the word **missing** mean?

   lost   asked

2. What does the word **hurried** mean?

   rushed   sleep

3. What does the word **delighted** mean?

   scared   happy

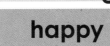

89

Make an inference

Readers **make an inference** when they use what they already know and clues in the text to figure out something.

It is important to make inferences, because authors don't always tell the reader everything they need to know.

1 Read the sentence. Decide which answer matches it.

1. José bought a tent, a sleeping bag, and a fishing rod.
   - ○ He is going to play a soccer game.
   - ○ He is going camping.

2. Rex has a party hat on his head.
   - ○ It is Rex's birthday.
   - ○ It is Rex's first day of school.

3. There are dark clouds in the sky.
   - ○ It is a sunny day.
   - ○ It is about to rain.

4. The dog has a stick in his mouth.
   - ○ The dog wants to play fetch.
   - ○ The dog wants to go to sleep.

Prepositions

A **preposition** can tell the location of a noun. **On**, **beside**, and **in front of** are prepositions.

1 Help complete the treasure map by following the directions below. Pay close attention to the prepositions in bold.

∧∧∧ Draw three shark fins **in** the ocean.

⩕⩕ Draw trees **next to** Alligator Swamp.

✗ Put an ✗ **between** the mountains.

Add a treasure chest **under** the ✗.

≋ Draw a river **above** the mountains.

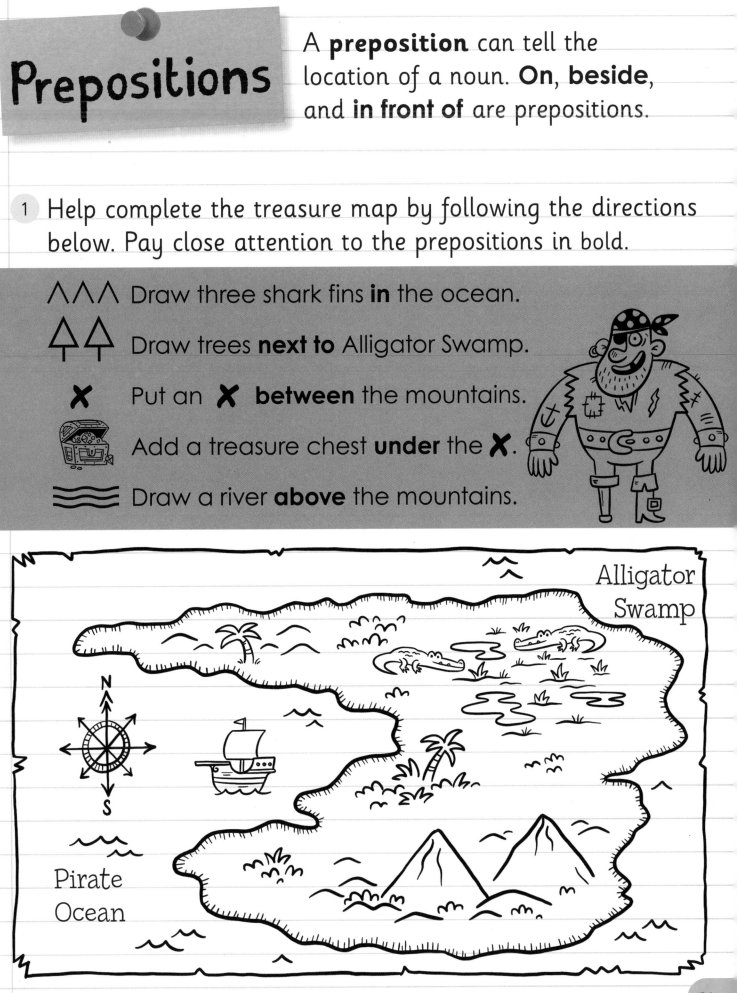

3-letter blends

Blends are two or three letters that keep their individual sounds when together.

Say each word aloud first.

1 Circle the correct 3-letter blend.

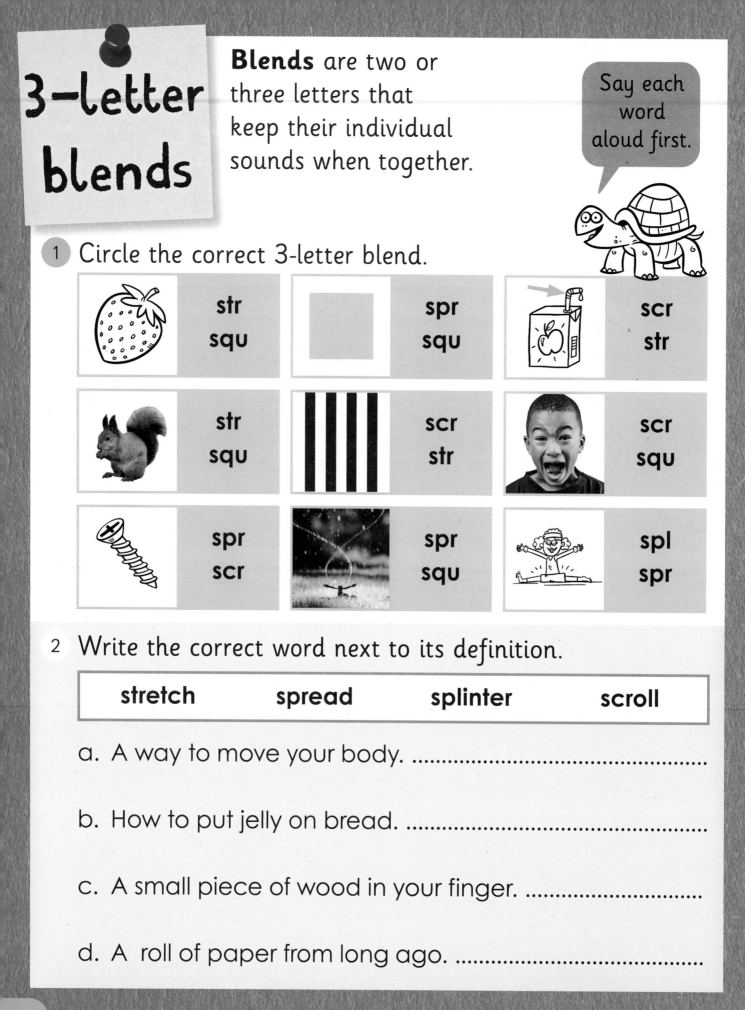

str / squ (strawberry)	spr / squ (blank square)	scr / str (juice box)
str / squ (squirrel)	scr / str (stripes)	scr / squ (screaming face)
spr / scr (screw)	spr / squ (sprinkler)	spl / spr (person splashing)

2 Write the correct word next to its definition.

stretch	spread	splinter	scroll

a. A way to move your body. ....

b. How to put jelly on bread. ....

c. A small piece of wood in your finger. ....

d. A roll of paper from long ago. ....

③ Complete the crossword puzzle by filling in the missing 3-letter blends to complete each word.

str	scr	squ	thr	spr	spl

Cross out the blends as you go!

④ Write two sentences choosing at least one word with a 3-letter blend from Activity 3.

1. ....
....

2. ....
....

Plan a non-fiction text

Writers think about ideas before choosing what to write about.

1 Write a list of animals that you might like to write about.

....

....

....

....

....

....

2 Now circle the animal you would like to write about. This will be your topic for Activity 3.

3 Writers research their topics. Write the answers to the questions that you already know. Then ask an adult to help you research the other answers.

To research means to find out more about something.

What is the animal's name?..

What does it look like?..

What does it eat?..

Where does it live?...

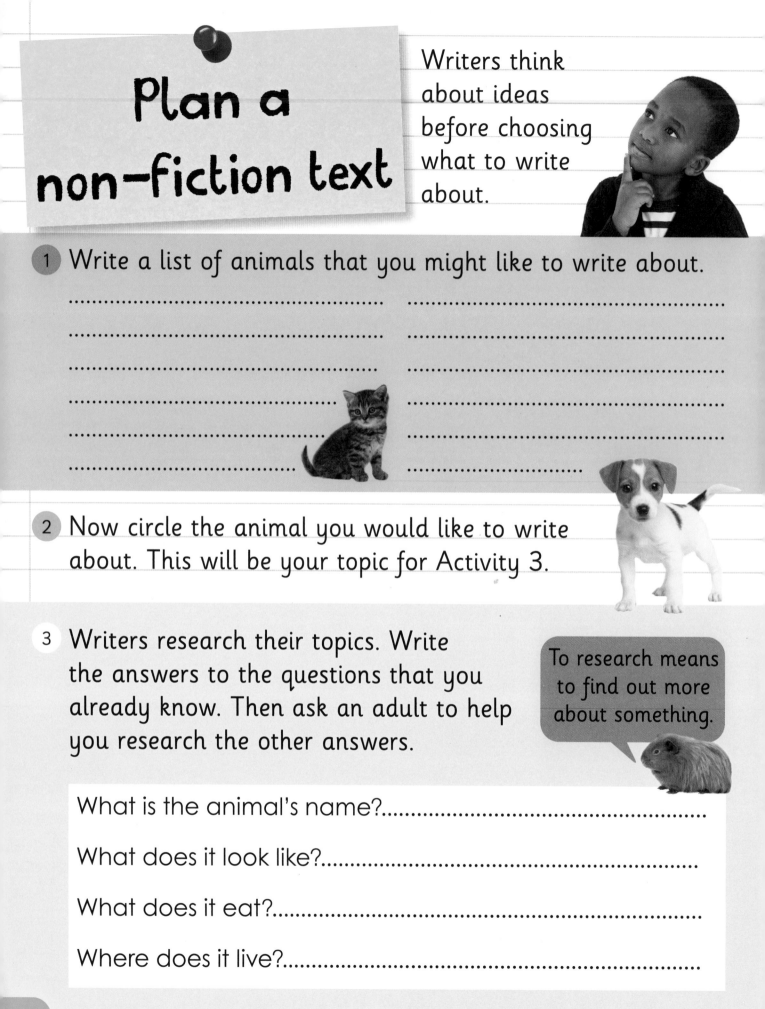

Write a non-fiction text

The first sentence is called a **topic sentence**. This tells the reader about the topic.

1 Use your research from the previous page to write about your animal. Be sure to start with a topic sentence.

....
....
....
....
....
....
....
....
....
....

2 Draw a picture of your animal.

Be sure to include its habitat. This is where an animal lives.

"R" – controlled vowels

When the letter "r" comes after a vowel, it changes the sound the vowel makes.

This is sometimes called **Bossy R**, as the "r" takes over and changes the vowel sound.

1 Read the "**ar**" words aloud.
Complete each sentence with the correct "**ar**" word.

shark	car	star	bark

a. Cherry the dog has a loud ....

b. An ocean is the habitat for a ....

c. Did you know that the sun is a ....?

d. The .... goes very fast.

2 Draw a line from each "**or**" word to the correct picture.

corn	north	fork

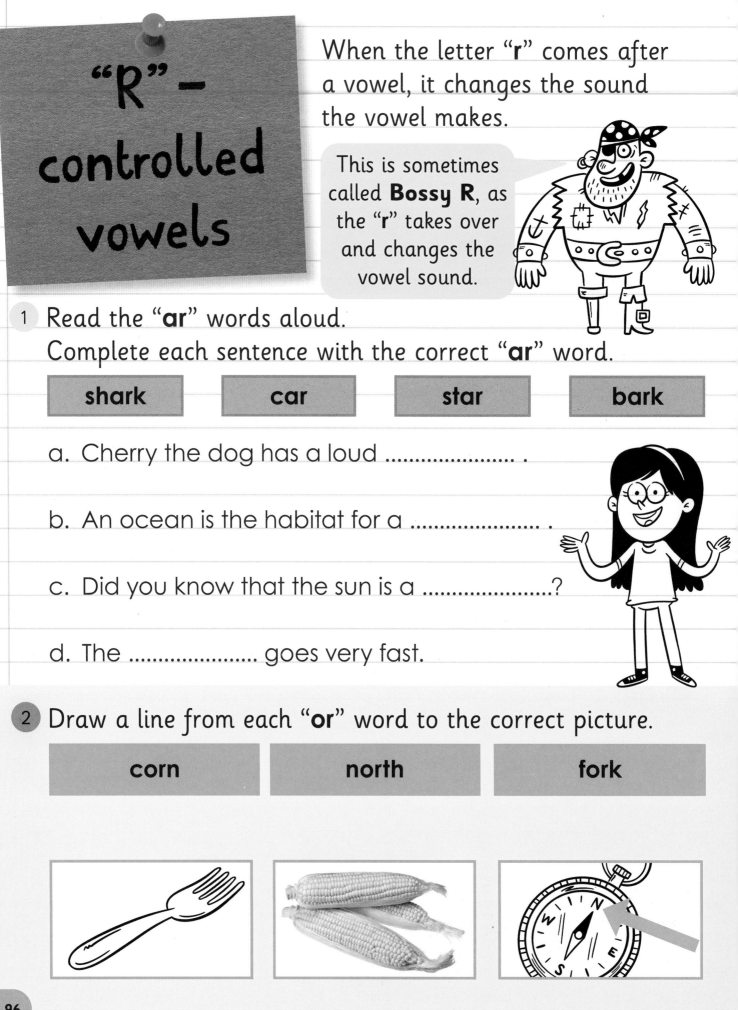

3 Draw a line from each "**er**" word to the correct picture.

butter	tiger	person	hammer

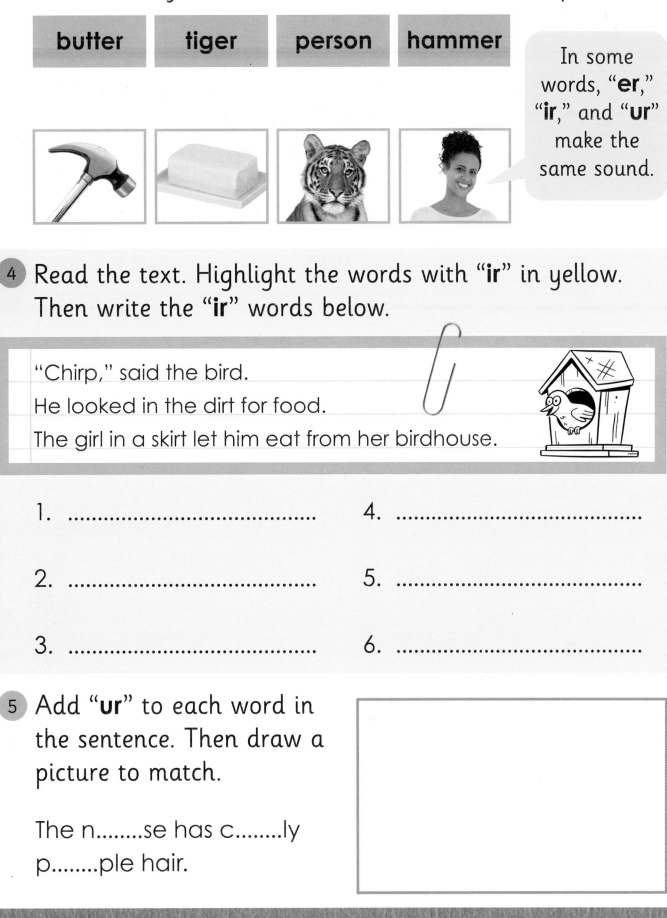

In some words, "**er**," "**ir**," and "**ur**" make the same sound.

4 Read the text. Highlight the words with "**ir**" in yellow. Then write the "**ir**" words below.

"Chirp," said the bird.

He looked in the dirt for food.

The girl in a skirt let him eat from her birdhouse.

1. ....   4. ....

2. ....   5. ....

3. ....   6. ....

5 Add "**ur**" to each word in the sentence. Then draw a picture to match.

The n........se has c........ly p........ple hair.

Compound words

A **compound word** is when two words are put together to make a bigger word.

Some compound words are **"inside," "blueberry,"** and **"cowboy."**

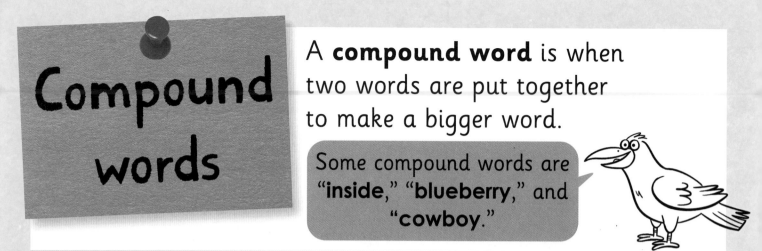

1 Make a compound word using one of the words below.

book	corn	ring

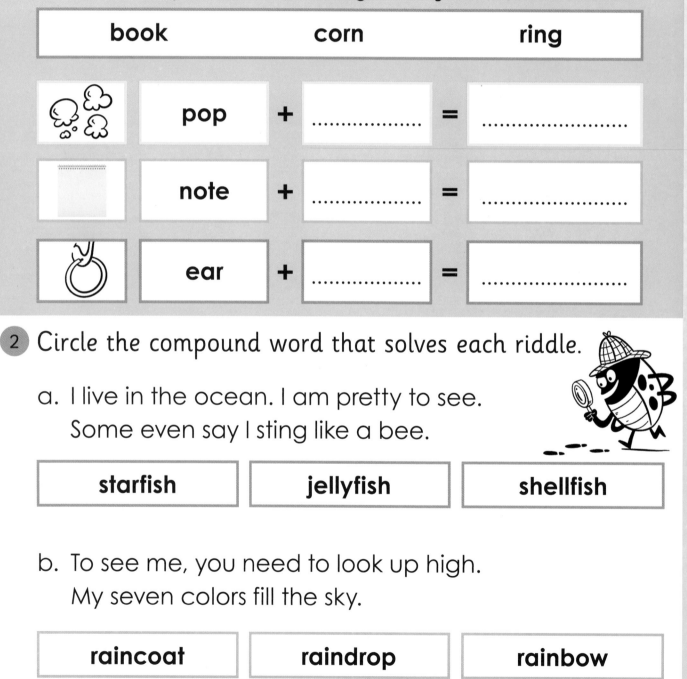

pop + ... = ...

note + ... = ...

ear + ... = ...

2 Circle the compound word that solves each riddle.

a. I live in the ocean. I am pretty to see.
   Some even say I sting like a bee.

starfish	jellyfish	shellfish

b. To see me, you need to look up high.
   My seven colors fill the sky.

raincoat	raindrop	rainbow

Point of view

Point of view is the view from which a story is told. A story can be told by the author, a character, or a narrator.

> A **narrator** is a storyteller who is not a character in the story.

1 Read about the different points of view.

Point of view	Who is telling the story	Key words
First person point of view	The story is told by one of the characters.	I, me, we
Second person point of view	The story is told by the author of the text. The author speaks to the reader.	you
Third person point of view	The story is told by a narrator who is not part of the story.	he, she, they

2 Read the sentences. Choose which point of view is being used.

> Use the key words to help you select the point of view.

I am so excited to go to the woods tomorrow.	1st	2nd	3rd
The fairies were so happy that they hugged each other tightly.	1st	2nd	3rd
Are you afraid of the dark?	1st	2nd	3rd

Author's point

Sometimes **authors** have a message that they are trying to prove.

This is called the **author's point**.

1. Olivia wrote about homework. Read her writing.

"No Homework" by Olivia

Kids should not have to do homework. When we get home, we need to spend time with family. We also need time to do other things like sports and music. Grown-ups do not have to do homework. That is not fair. These are the reasons kids should not have to do homework.

2. Answer these questions.
   1. Who is the author of the paper? ....
   2. What is the author's point? ....
      ....
   3. What is one reason that the author gives? ....
      ....
      ....
   4. What is another reason that the author gives? ....
      ....
   5. Do you agree with the author? ....
      ....
      Why? ....
      ....
      ....

Text features

Text features help readers better understand the text.

1 Read to find out about a few text features.

A **table of contents** tells the sections or chapters in the book and their page numbers.

A **glossary** tells the definition of special words in the book.

A **heading** tells when a new section begins and what that section is about.

A **caption** is a sentence near a picture or photograph. It tells about the picture or photograph.

A **chart** neatly shows information.

2 Read the table of contents. Then answer the questions.

Table of contents

Is this book fiction or non-fiction?

1. What page can you learn about tornadoes? ....

2. How many chapters are in this book? ....

3. What page can you find definitions for important words? ....

4. What will you learn about on page 8? ....

Conjunctions

A **conjunction** is a word that connects two words or phrases. Some conjunctions are: **and**, **but**, **or**, **so**, **because**.

1 Connect the words using the given conjunction. Write the phrase on the line.

and
in	out

.... in and out ....

| back | forth |

....

| this | that |

....

or
right	wrong

....

| hot | cold |

....

| truth | dare |

....

2 Say each conjunction aloud. Complete each sentence by writing the missing conjunction.

a. We like to play chess .... checkers.

b. You might win .... lose.

c. Jason wants to finish the puzzle, ... there is a missing piece.

Word bank
but
and
or

3 Read the text. Underline the joining words.

> The music played and we walked around the chairs.
> There were two of us but only one chair. Would Sam or I win?
> The music stopped, so we stopped walking.
> Then I sat down on the chair and I was the winner!

4 Write the conjunctions that you underlined.

1. ....

2. ....

3. ....

4. ....

5. ....

> Remember: **and, but, or, so, because** are all joining words.

5 Complete the sentences below. Remember to add a conjunction to link the phrases together.

a. We should play more games at school [................] **conjunction**

....

b. Hide-and-seek is fun to play [................] .... **conjunction**

....

Compound sentences

A **compound sentence** is when two or more sentences are combined with a comma and a conjunction. **For example:**

I like the color red,	but	orange is my favorite color.
1st sentence	joining word	2nd sentence

1 Read each pair of sentences.
  Draw a circle around the compound sentence in each pair.

a I like to go to the library.
  I like to go to the library, and I read books there.

b The vet takes care of my dog.
  The vet takes care of my dog, and she gives him medicine.

c The market is open today, but it will be closed tomorrow.
  The market is closed tomorrow.

2 Make a compound sentence by joining the sentences together.

The second sentence starts with a lowercase letter when sentences are combined.

I went to the dentist. I got a new toothbrush.
...................................., and ....

Today is a holiday. The mail carrier did not come.
.... so ....

Irregular words

Many sight words have **irregular spellings**. These words are not spelled like they sound. That is one reason they should be recognized quickly by sight.

1 Read the irregular sight words.
Write the correct word to complete each sentence.

great	school	laugh	was

a. Your jokes make me ....
b. My .... has a lot of books for kids.
c. Harvey had a .... time dancing with his friends.
d. The apple .... sweet and juicy.

2 Practice spelling and writing each sight word.

Say the word	Spell the word	Write the word
great	g-r-e-a-t	
school	s-c-h-o-o-l	
laugh	l-a-u-g-h	
was	w-a-s	

Base words

A **base word** is a word that can stand alone. A base word can be changed by adding letters to the beginning or the end of the word.

1 Find and highlight the base word in yellow.

Base word	Highlight the base word	
wash	washing	rewash
play	playful	playing
hope	hoped	hopeful
call	recalled	calling
ring	ringing	rings
new	newest	renew

2 Draw a line to match each word to its base word.

Base word

fish　　　　　　　restful

quiet　　　　　　runner

tie　　　　　　　fishing

rest　　　　　　quietly

able　　　　　　untie

run　　　　　　unable

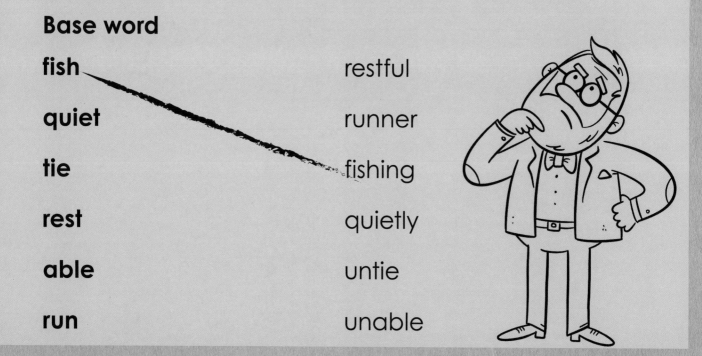

Inflectional endings

Inflectional endings are letters added to the end of a word to change its meaning. To add "**ed**" means something has already happened. To add "**ing**" means something is happening now.

1 Fill in the chart. Read each word aloud.

Base word	Add "ed" Past tense	Add "ing" Present tense
cook	cooked	cooking
jump		
talk		
clean		

2 The inflectional ending "**ed**" can have many sounds. It can sound like /**t**/ in "**looked**."
It can sound like /**d**/ in "**played**."
It can sound like /**id**/ in "**wanted**."
Read the word. Check the sound that you hear for "**ed**."

fixed	/**t**/	/**d**/	/**id**/
loved	/**t**/	/**d**/	/**id**/
wanted	/**t**/	/**d**/	/**id**/
closed	/**t**/	/**d**/	/**id**/
waited	/**t**/	/**d**/	/**id**/
worked	/**t**/	/**d**/	/**id**/

Commas

A **comma** is a mark used to separate a series or a group of three or more things. A comma is also used to separate the day from the year in a date.

Series: I like to jump, skip, and hop.

Date: January 1, 2023

January 1, 2023

1. Add a comma to the dates below.

> March 15 1995
> September 7 2021
> February 14 2022
> August 13 1983
> June 2 2004
> October 31 2010

2. Write your birthday using a comma correctly.

I was born on

....

....

....

3. Are commas used correctly in the series of items? Circle the sentences that are correct.

a. My favorite colors are black, white, and green.

b. My best, friends are Annie Janiya and Marcus.

c. She bought apples, pears, and bananas.

d. I am kind, funny, and, loving.

Prefixes

A **prefix** is a group of letters that can be added to the front of a word to change its meaning. For example, the prefix "**re**" usually means "**again**."

1 Use the prefix and base word to figure out the meaning of the word in bold. Write the meaning of each word.

	prefix + base word	meaning
reread	re+read	read again
refill	re+fill	
rewrite	re+write	

2 Use the prefix and base word to figure out the meaning of the word in bold. Write the meaning of each word.

	prefix + base word	meaning
unkind	un+kind	not kind
unfair	un+fair	
unhappy	un+happy	

The prefix "**un**" usually means "**not**."

Suffixes

A **suffix** is a group of letters that can be added to the end of a word to change its meaning. For example, the suffix "**ful**" usually means "**full of**."

"**Careful**" means to be full of care.

1 Circle the words that have a suffix.

a. The dog is playful
b. This is helpful.
c. It was painful when I fell.
d. Kisha is so cheerful.

2 The words below have the suffix "**ly**." Read the words aloud. Draw a line to match each word to its correct meaning.

The suffix "**ly**" usually means "**how it is done**."

quickly	in a way that is safe
weekly	in a way that is quick
lovely	in a way that is loved
safely	done every week

3 Read each sentence. Choose the correct suffix. The suffix "**less**" means to be without.

a. Shh! Don't talk so loud........ . (**ly, ful**)
b. That snake is friendly and harm........... . (**ly, less**)
c. The parrot is pretty. It is so color........ . (**ly, ful**)

Prefixes and suffixes

Prefixes are groups of letters that can be added to the **beginning** of a word to change its meaning. **Suffixes** are groups of letters that are added to the **end** of a word to change its meaning.

1 Do these words have a prefix or a suffix? Check the correct answer.

remove	prefix ◯	suffix ◯
singer	prefix ◯	suffix ◯
teacher	prefix ◯	suffix ◯
preschool	prefix ◯	suffix ◯

2 The words below have a prefix or a suffix.
Circle the words that have a prefix.
Underline the words with a suffix.

player	**pretest**	**farmer**	**kindness**	**precook**
unsafe	**seller**	**rename**	**retell**	**fastest**

3 These words have the same suffix: farm**er**, teach**er**, play**er**. Write two more words with the suffix "**er**."

1. ....

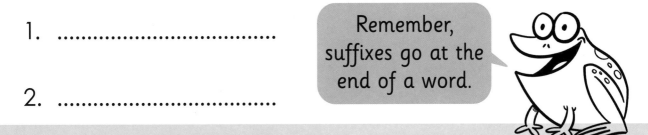

Remember, suffixes go at the end of a word.

2. ....

Make a timeline

A timeline shows important events in order by date.

> A timeline can use years, months, days, or hours.

1. Mae Jemison has been a doctor and an astronaut. Read the timeline about Mae Jemison's life.

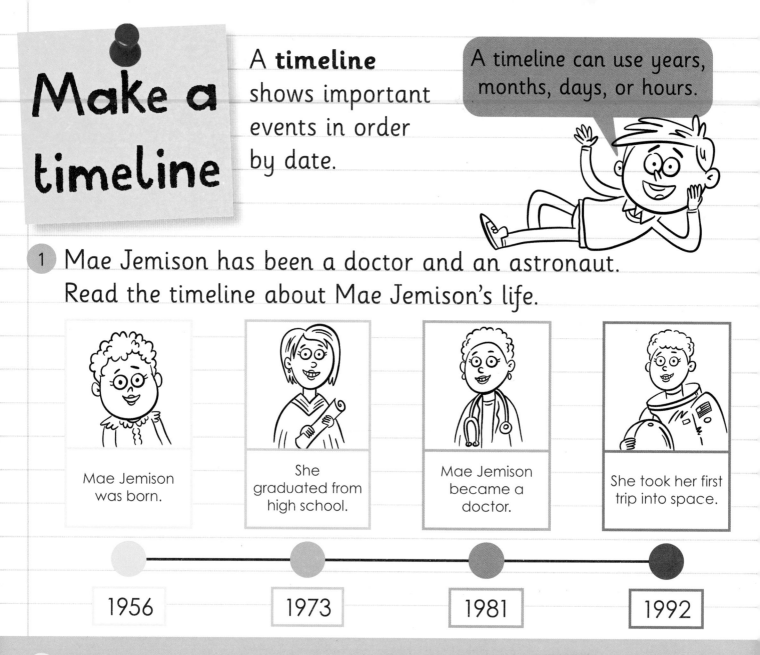

| Mae Jemison was born. | She graduated from high school. | Mae Jemison became a doctor. | She took her first trip into space. |

1956 — 1973 — 1981 — 1992

2. Make a timeline about your life. Write important events and the year they happened on the timeline.

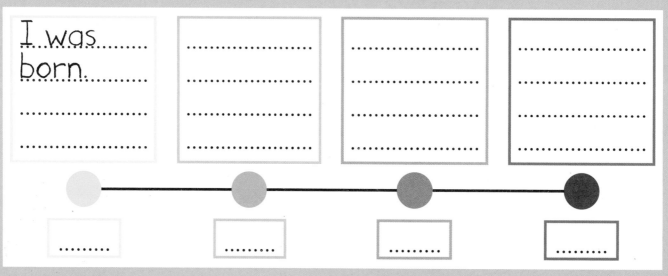

I was born. .... | .... | .... | ....

.... | .... | .... | ....

Plan a narrative

A **narrative** tells a story. Writers make a plan before they write a story.

1. Think of something you did that was exciting or difficult. Make a list of those things.

1. ....

2. ....

3. ....

Circle the idea that you like best. This is the topic for your narrative.

2. Plan for your story. Answer each of the questions using words or phrases.

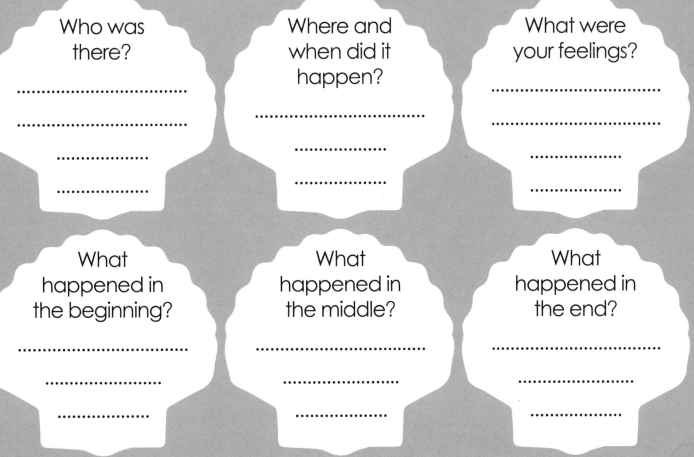

Who was there?
....
....
....
....

Where and when did it happen?
....
....
....

What were your feelings?
....
....
....
....

What happened in the beginning?
....
....
....

What happened in the middle?
....
....
....

What happened in the end?
....
....
....

Make a draft

Writers will often make a **first draft**. The first draft of your story does not have to be perfect. You will make it better later.

Remember to use temporal words like "**next**" and "**then**."

1. Write the first draft of your story. Use your notes from the previous page to help you.

2. Read your story aloud. Follow the steps below to revise and edit your work.

1. Make sure each sentence starts with a capital letter.
2. Make sure each sentence ends with the correct punctuation mark.
3. Circle the tricky words. Get help from an adult to fix the spelling of the tricky words.
4. Reread the story. Fix any parts that do not make sense.

Write a narrative

Writers make a **final version** of their stories to share with others.

1 Write the final version of your story. Make sure you include any changes that you made to make it better.

2 Draw a picture for your story.

Write an opinion

An **opinion** tells what you think or how you feel about a topic. People have different opinions.

1 Gloria thinks that pineapples are the best fruit. Read her opinion below.

"The Best Dessert" by Gloria

I think pineapples are the best fruit. Pineapples are the best because they are so sweet. They taste good as juice too. Pineapples can be eaten for dessert. That is why yummy pineapples are the best!

2 What is the best dessert? Share your opinion by responding below.

The best dessert is

....

It is the best because

....

....

....

3 Draw a picture of your favorite dessert.

Write a letter

A **letter** is a written message usually sent in the mail.

A pen pal is a person you get to know by writing letters.

1 Read the letter below.

Dear human,

Greetings from the planet Splog! My name is Glug and I am six years old. My planet is very pretty. There are lots of purple brees. What color are the brees on your planet?

I live with my mom and grandad in Splogville. We like to go fishing for flugs and weets. Yummy!

From, Scrup

2 Can you write a letter back to Scrup telling the alien all about yourself?

Dear ....,

I live in ....

I live with ....

My family likes to ....

....

....

From, ...
        Your name

Answers

Page 4-5

Write letters A–M

Uppercase letters are also called **capital letters**.

There are 26 letters in the alphabet. Each letter has **uppercase** and **lowercase** forms.

1 Trace and write the uppercase and lowercase letters.

A AAAA	a aaaa	F FFFF	f fffff
B BBBB	b bbbb	G GGGG	g ggggg
C CCCC	c cccc	H HHHH	h hhhh
D DDDD	d dddd	I IIIII	i iiiii
E EEEE	e eeee	J JJJJ	j jjjj
		K KKKK	k kkkk
		L LLLLL	l lllll
		M MMMM	m mmmm

Page 6-7

Write letters N–Z

Can you think of any words that begin with these letters?

1 Trace and write the uppercase and lowercase letters.

N NNNN	n nnnn	S SSSS	s ssss
O OOOO	o oooo	T TTTT	t ttttt
P PPPP	p pppp	U UUUU	u uuuu
Q QQQQ	q qqqq	V VVVV	v vvvv
R RRRR	r rrrrr	W WWWW	w wwww
		X XXXX	x xxxx
		Y YYYY	y yyyy
		Z ZZZZ	z zzzz

Page 8-9

Nature abc

1 Fill in the missing lowercase letters.

a b c d e f g h i
j k l m n o p q r
s t u v w x y z

2 Following the example, write the words in **alphabetical order** on the lines below.

moth   ant   snail   bee

1. ant
2. bee
3. moth
4. snail

Use the first letter of each word to help put them in abc order.

All about me

1 Write your first name and last name. Then draw a picture of yourself in the frame.

Don't forget to use an uppercase letter for the first letter of your first name and your last name.

My name is
ANSWERS WILL VARY

DRAWINGS WILL VARY

2 Answer each question.

My favorite food is
ANSWERS WILL VARY

My favorite color is
ANSWERS WILL VARY

My birthday is in the month of
ANSWERS WILL VARY

Page 10-11

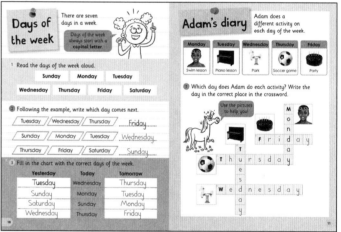

Days of the week

There are seven days in a week.

Days of the week always start with a **capital letter**.

1 Read the days of the week aloud.

Sunday   Monday   Tuesday
Wednesday   Thursday   Friday   Saturday

2 Following the example, write which day comes next.

Tuesday	Wednesday	Thursday	Friday
Sunday	Monday	Tuesday	Wednesday
Thursday	Friday	Saturday	Sunday

3 Fill in the chart with the correct days of the week.

Yesterday	Today	Tomorrow
Tuesday	Wednesday	Thursday
Sunday	Monday	Tuesday
Saturday	Sunday	Monday
Wednesday	Thursday	Friday

Adam's diary

Adam does a different activity on each day of the week.

Monday	Tuesday	Wednesday	Thursday	Friday
Swim lesson	Piano lesson	Park	Soccer game	Party

1 Which day does Adam do each activity? Write the day in the correct place in the crossword.

Use the pictures to help you!

M o n
F r i d a y
T
T h u r s d a y
e
s
W e d n e s d a y
a
y

Page 12-13

What is "I"?

"I" can be a letter or a word.

Always use a **capital letter** when writing "I" as a word.

1 Read the text. Circle the word "I" in each sentence.

I like bears.
I like parrots.
I like monkeys.
I do not like snakes!

2 Color the word "I" pink. Color the word "me" green.

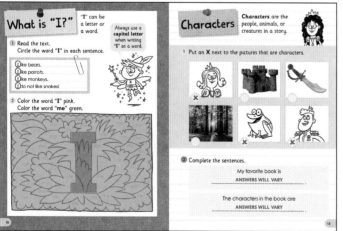

Characters

Characters are the people, animals, or creatures in a story.

1 Put an X next to the pictures that are characters.

2 Complete the sentences.

My favorite book is
ANSWERS WILL VARY

The characters in the book are
ANSWERS WILL VARY

Page 14-15

Create a character

Every story has a **main character**. The main character is the person or animal that the story is mostly about.

Argh! I'm Captain Toby, a scary pirate.

1 Create a character by filling in the blanks.

My character's name is ANSWERS WILL VARY
My character lives in ANSWERS WILL VARY
My character likes to ANSWERS WILL VARY

2 Circle three words that describe your character.

| kind | noisy | bossy | brave | clumsy |
| happy | wild | loving | shy | funny |

ANSWERS WILL VARY

3 Draw a picture of your character, then write their description.

DRAWINGS WILL VARY

ANSWERS WILL VARY

Compare characters

Compare means to find things that are similar or different.

Readers can compare characters in a story.

1 Read the story below.

Tom and May sat down to eat lunch.
Tom opened his lunch box. "Yes, I love my lunch!"
May opened her lunch box. "Oh no!" she said.
Tom started to eat his fruit. He saw that May was sad.
"Do you want some grapes?" he asked.
May smiled. "Yes, please," she said.
"I have strawberries, but I don't like them." "I like strawberries!" said Tom.
May and Tom shared their grapes and strawberries.

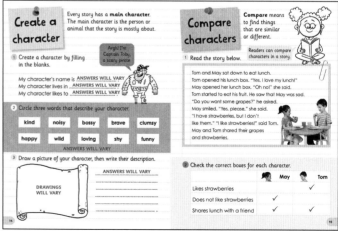

2 Check the correct boxes for each character.

	May	Tom
Likes strawberries		✓
Does not like strawberries	✓	
Shares lunch with a friend	✓	✓

Page 16-17

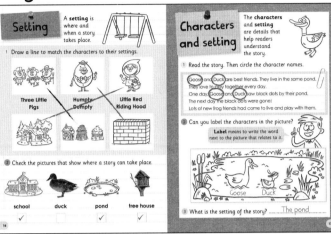

Page 18-19

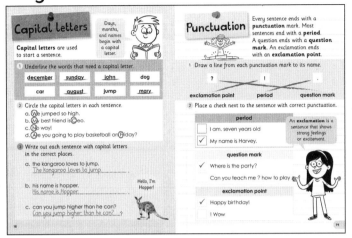

Page 20-21

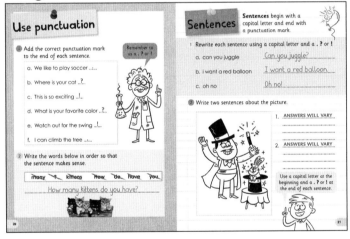

Page 22-23

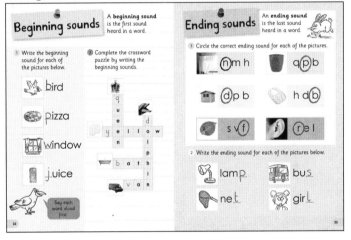

Page 24-25

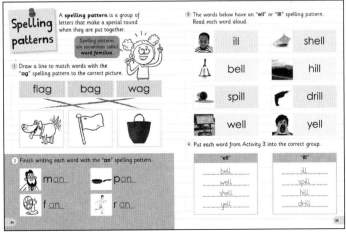

Page 26-27

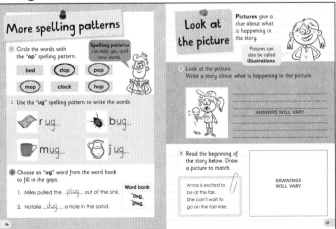

Answers

Page 28-29

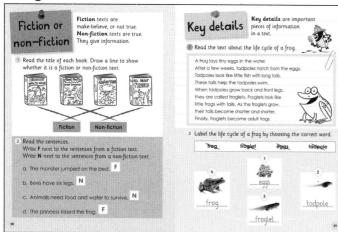

Page 30-31

Page 32-33

Page 34-35

Page 36-37

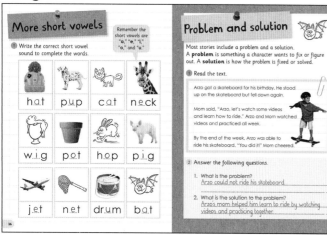

Page 38-39

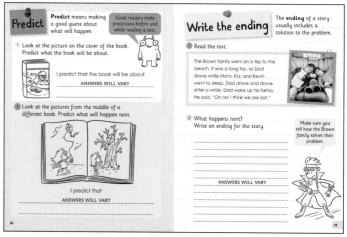

Page 40-41

Adjectives

Adjectives are words that describe a person, place, or thing.

I am a big monster!

① Circle the adjectives.

(big) (small) (green)
dinosaur (old) ball
(fast) (tasty) (soft)
(loud) baby truck

② Choosing from the words below, write the adjective that best describes each dinosaur picture.

spotted   spiky   tiny

spiky   spotted   tiny

③ Think of an adjective to describe each picture. Write it below.

ANSWERS WILL VARY   ANSWERS WILL VARY   ANSWERS WILL VARY

④ Read the adjectives in the word bank aloud. Then add in the adjectives to complete the story.
ANSWERS WILL VARY

Word bank
yellow
shiny
cold
new
blue

It was a ___cold___ night. Mom told Dino to put on his _____ jacket.
"No! I want to wear my _____ raincoat," said Dino. "I like my _____ raincoat the best." "Okay," said Mom. "Make sure you wear your _____ rain boots, too."

⑤ Circle the adjective in each sentence.
a. The dinosaur walked across the (green) grass.
b. That is a (beautiful) waterfall.
c. Some dinosaurs ate leaves from (tall) trees.
d. Some dinosaurs had (pointy) teeth.

Page 42-43

Shape poems

A **shape poem** is a poem in the shape of an object. The words and phrases used in the poem usually describe that object.

① Read the shape poem about pizza.

Soft golden crust.
Ooey-gooey yellow cheese.
Sweet, juicy pineapple.
Spicy sauce, please!
Get it while it's hot.
Perfect pizza.
Munch!
Yum!

② Which words from the pizza poem relate to the five senses? Write them below.

ANSWERS WILL VARY

👁 _____
✋ _____
👂 _____
👃 _____
👅 _____

③ Write a shape poem about ice cream. Use words or phrases to describe ice cream in your poem.

ANSWERS WILL VARY

Use some words that connect to your five senses.

④ Which words in your ice cream poem connect to the five senses? Write them below.

Sight	Touch	Sound	Smell	Taste
ANSWERS WILL VARY				

Page 44-45

Beginning blends

Blends are two or three letters that keep their own sounds when put together.

Blends can be at the **beginning** of a word.

① Color in the correct beginning blend for each picture.

gl / fl   gl / bl   bl / gl
gl / gl   cl / pl   pl / gl

② Can you match each of these words to an example?

plus	gloves	black	climb

| Something to keep your hands warm | Go up | using your hands and feet | |
| gloves | plus | climb | black |

③ Choose the correct "br" or "pr" blend for each word.

br_oom   pr_esent   pr_ice
br_ead   br_ush   pr_ize

④ Choose the correct "gr" or "cr" blend for each word.

cr_ab   cr_ane   gr_een
gr_apes   cr_ow   gr_in

Page 46-47

More beginning blends

① Fill in the correct blend to complete the words.

sp_onge   sw_ing
sn_ail   sc_arf

② Choose the correct blend to fill in the gaps.

Try each blend out first.

I can sm_ell the sk_unk.   (sm/sw) (sl/sk)

I like to ride my sc_ooter.   (sc/sn)

Do you know how to sk_i in the sn_ow?   (sk/st) (sm/sn)

Retell

Retell means to tell the important parts of the story, including characters, setting, beginning, middle, and end.

① Read the text.

Jo and Akim went to the park to play soccer. Akim brought his ball. They started to play. Jo took a shot at the goal. She kicked the ball hard. Oh no! The ball shot over the fence and into a yard. Akim ran to the fence. A man was in the yard. He picked up the ball and gave it to Akim. "Thank you," said Akim. Jo and Akim started to play again.

② Who are the characters?
1. Jo
2. Akim
3. A man

③ Where is the setting?
The park and yard

④ Write what happened at the beginning, in the middle, and at the end of the story.

Beginning	Middle	End
ANSWERS WILL VARY	ANSWERS WILL VARY	ANSWERS WILL VARY

Page 48-49

Main topic

The **main topic** describes what the text is mostly about.

① Read the text.

Plants have many parts. Each plant part has a special job.
Roots hold the plant in the ground. They help plants get water and food to live.
The **stem** holds the plant up. It also helps carry water and food through the plant.
The **leaves** use water, air, and sunlight to make food.
The **flowers** bring insects that help the plant grow seeds.
The **seeds** can grow into new plants.

② What is the main topic of the text? Circle the correct answer.
a. Animal parts
b. Plant parts
c. Body parts

Check the text for your answer.

③ Use the bold words from the text to help label the parts of a plant.

seeds   flower
leaves   stem
roots

Sort words

Words can be sorted into **groups** or categories to show a connection.

① Write each word in the correct group.

piano   doll   violin   robot
drum   ball   flute   teddy bear

🧸 Toys	🎷 Instruments
doll	piano
robot	violin
ball	drum
teddy bear	flute

② Read the words in each category. Write a name to describe each category.

paints or colors	fruits
red yellow	kiwi mango
green pink	watermelon pear

③ Write four words for the category "clothes."

ANSWERS WILL VARY

Page 50-51

Sight words

Sight words are common words found in text. They should be recognized quickly by sight.

① Read and trace each sight word. Then write each word in two colors.

Read the word	Trace the word	Write the word in two different colors	
of	of	of	of
give	give	give	give
put	put	put	put
were	were	were	were

② Find each of the sight words in the word search.

Sight words are also called high-frequency words or tricky words.

p w e r e g
x v o p w i
m p u t g v
g y r o f t

☑ of
☑ give
☑ put
☑ were

More sight words

① Read and trace each sight word. Then write each word in two colors.

Read the word	Trace the word	Write the word in two different colors	
her	her	her	her
walk	walk	walk	walk
again	again	again	again
know	know	know	know

② Circle the correct letters to spell each sight word.

her   m h (i) a (e) (r) f s
walk   (w) i (a) (l) (k) c
again   (a) j (g) (a) (i) (n) m
know   l (k) (n) (o) u (w) x

Answers

Page 52-53

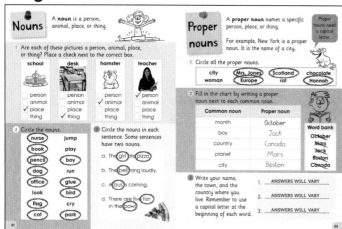

Page 54-55

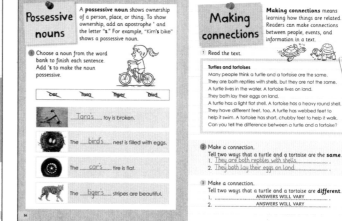

Page 56-57

Page 58-59

Page 60-61

Page 62-63

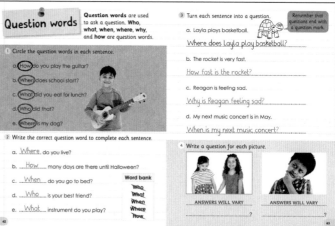

Page 64-65

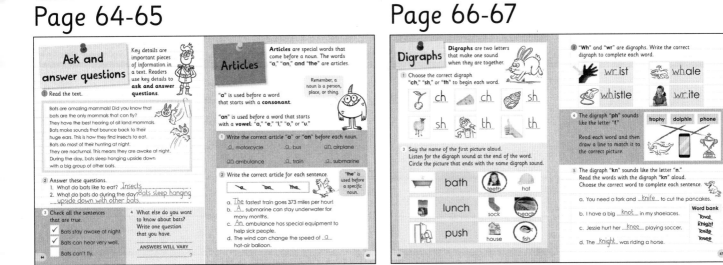

Ask and answer questions

Key details are important pieces of information in a text. Readers use key details to **ask and answer questions.**

① Read the text.

Bats are amazing mammals! Did you know that bats are the only mammals that can fly?
They have the best hearing of all land mammals.
Bats make sounds that bounce back to their huge ears. This is how they find insects to eat.
Bats do most of their hunting at night.
They are nocturnal. This means they are awake at night.
During the day, bats sleep hanging upside down with a big group of other bats.

② Answer these questions.
1. What do bats like to eat? Insects
2. What do bats do during the day? Bats sleep hanging upside down with other bats.

③ Check all the sentences that are true.
☑ Bats stay awake at night.
☑ Bats can hear very well.
☐ Bats can't fly.

④ What else do you want to know about bats? Write one question that you have.
ANSWERS WILL VARY

Articles

Articles are special words that come before a noun. The words **"a," "an,"** and **"the"** are articles.

Remember, a noun is a person, place, or thing.

"a" is used before a word that starts with a **consonant.**

"an" is used before a word that starts with a **vowel: "a," "e," "i," "o,"** or **"u"**

① Write the correct article **"a"** or **"an"** before each noun.
a. motorcycle   a. bus   an. airplane
an. ambulance   a. train   a. submarine

② Write the correct article for each sentence.
a   an   the
"the" is used before a specific noun.

a. The fastest train goes 373 miles per hour!
b. A submarine can stay underwater for many months.
c. An ambulance has special equipment to help sick people.
d. The wind can change the speed of a hot-air balloon.

Page 66-67

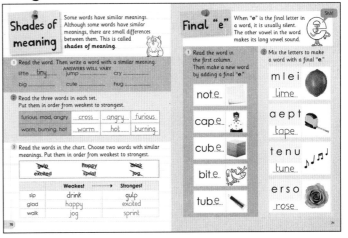

Digraphs

Digraphs are two letters that make one sound when they are together.

① Choose the correct digraph "ch," "sh," or "th" to begin each word.
ch   ch   sh
sh   th   th

② Say the name of the first picture aloud. Listen for the digraph sound at the end of the word. Circle the picture that ends with the same digraph sound.
bath — teeth, hat
lunch — sock, beach
push — house, fish

③ "Wh" and "wr" are digraphs. Write the correct digraph to complete each word.
wr.ist   wh.ale
wh.istle   wr.ite

④ The digraph "ph" sounds like the letter "f."
trophy   dolphin   phone
Read each word and then draw a line to match it to the correct picture.

⑤ The digraph "kn" sounds like the letter "n." Read the words with the digraph "kn" aloud. Choose the correct word to complete each sentence.
a. You need a fork and knife to cut the pancakes.
b. I have a big knot in my shoelaces.
c. Jessie hurt her knee playing soccer.
d. The knight was riding a horse.

Word bank
knot
knight
knife
knee

Page 68-69

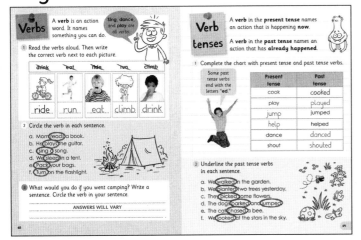

Verbs

A **verb** is an action word. It names something you can do.

Sing, dance, and play are all verbs.

① Read the verbs aloud. Then write the correct verb next to each picture.
drink   eat   ride   run   climb
ride   run   eat   climb   drink

② Circle the verb in each sentence.
a. Mom reads a book.
b. He plays the guitar.
c. Sing a song.
d. We sleep in a tent.
e. Pack your bags.
f. Turn on the flashlight.

③ What would you do if you went camping? Write a sentence. Circle the verb in your sentence.
ANSWERS WILL VARY

Verb tenses

A **verb** in the **present tense** names an action that is happening **now.**

A **verb** in the **past tense** names an action that has **already happened.**

① Complete the chart with present tense and past tense verbs.
Some past tense verbs end with the letters "ed."

Present tense	Past tense
cook	cooked
play	played
jump	jumped
help	helped
dance	danced
shout	shouted

② Underline the past tense verbs in each sentence.
a. We walked in the garden.
b. We planted two trees yesterday.
c. They picked some flowers.
d. The dog barked and jumped.
e. The cat chased a bee.
f. We looked at the stars in the sky.

Page 70-71

Shades of meaning

Some words have similar meanings. Although some words have similar meanings, there are small differences between them. This is called **shades of meaning.**

① Read the word. Then write a word with a similar meaning.
little tiny   jump   cry
big   cute   hug
ANSWERS WILL VARY

② Read the three words in each set. Put them in order from weakest to strongest.
furious, mad, angry — cross   angry   furious
warm, burning, hot — warm   hot   burning

③ Read the words in the chart. Choose two words with similar meanings. Put them in order from weakest to strongest.
gulp   happy   drink
excited   sprint

	Weakest →	Strongest
sip	drink	gulp
glad	happy	excited
walk	jog	sprint

Final "e"

When "e" is the final letter in a word, it is usually silent. The other vowel in the word makes its long vowel sound.

Shh!

① Read the word in the first column. Then make a new word by adding a final "e."
not.e.
cap.e.
cub.e.
bit.e.
tub.e.

② Mix the letters to make a word with a final "e."
m l e i → lime
a e p t → tape
t e n u → tune
e r s o → rose

Page 72-73

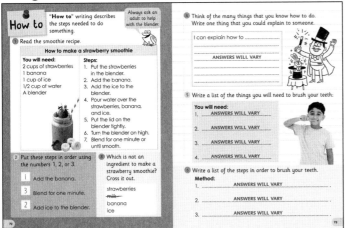

How to

"How to" writing describes the steps needed to do something you can do.

Always ask an adult to help with the blender.

① Read the smoothie recipe.

How to make a strawberry smoothie

You will need:
2 cups of strawberries
1 banana
1 cup of ice
1/2 cup of water
A blender

Steps:
1. Put the strawberries in the blender.
2. Add the banana.
3. Add the ice to the blender.
4. Pour water over the strawberries, banana, and ice.
5. Put the lid on the blender tightly.
6. Turn the blender on high.
7. Blend for one minute or until smooth.

② Put these steps in order using the numbers 1, 2, or 3.
1 Add the banana.
3 Blend for one minute.
2 Add ice to the blender.

③ Which is not an ingredient to make a strawberry smoothie? Cross it out.
strawberries
milk
banana
ice

④ Think of the many things that you know how to do. Write one thing that you could explain to someone.
I can explain how to
ANSWERS WILL VARY

⑤ Write a list of the things you will need to brush your teeth:
You will need:
1. ANSWERS WILL VARY
2. ANSWERS WILL VARY
3. ANSWERS WILL VARY
4. ANSWERS WILL VARY

⑥ Write a list of the steps in order to brush your teeth.
Method:
1. ANSWERS WILL VARY
2. ANSWERS WILL VARY
3. ANSWERS WILL VARY

Page 74-75

Long vowel "a"

The long "a" sound can be made using "ay" or "ai."

① Read each word aloud. Then write each word in the correct egg basket.
hay   tay   rain   tay   paid
play   tail   wait
rain   tail   hay   lay
wait   paid   ray   play
ai   ay

② Read the "ai" and "ay" words aloud. Find each word in the word search.
☑ nail
☑ away
☑ rainbow
☑ day

r	a	i	n	b	o	w
c	y	k	v	i	e	l
n	j	q	h	r	t	a
a	w	f	z	p	l	e
i	u	d	a	y	o	a
l	g	m	s	x	d	y

Long vowel "e"

The long "e" sound can be made using "ee," "ea," or "ey"

When two vowels work together, it is called a **vowel pattern** or a **vowel team.**

① Color the candy with the "ee" pattern red. Color the candy with the "ea" pattern yellow. Color the candy with the "ey" pattern green.
keep   each   peas   bees   eat
honey   cheek   peach   donkey   clean

② Read the words aloud. Add them to the story below.
teeth   treat   green   beans   sweets

I went to the candy store to get a treat.
My mom said too many sweets could hurt my teeth.
I got some jelly beans.
I like the green jelly beans the best.

123

Answers

Page 76-77

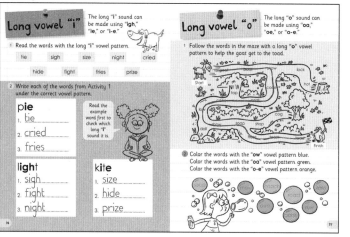

Page 78-79

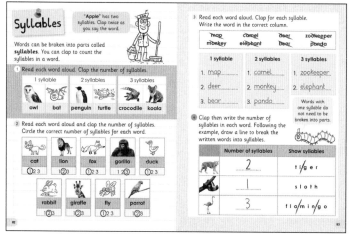

Page 80-81

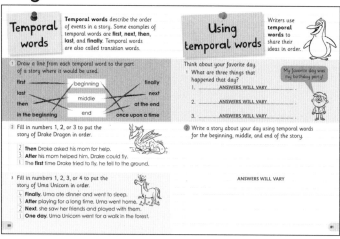

Page 82-83

Page 84-85

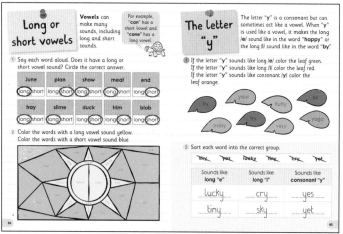

Page 86-87

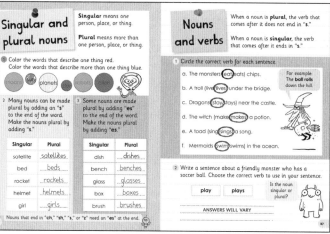

Page 88-89

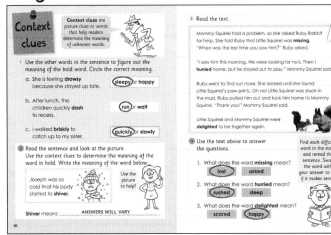

Page 90-91

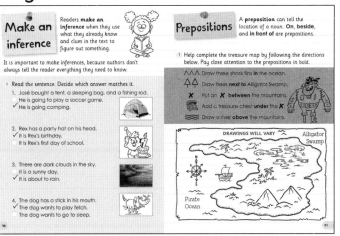

Page 92-93

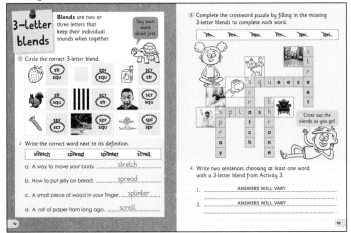

Page 94-95

Page 96-97

Page 98-99

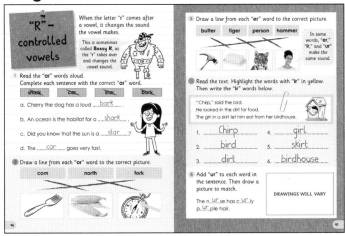

Answers

Page 100-101

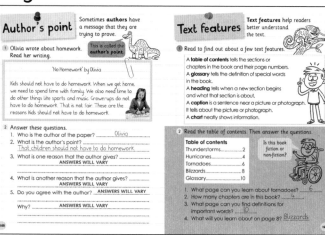

Page 102-103

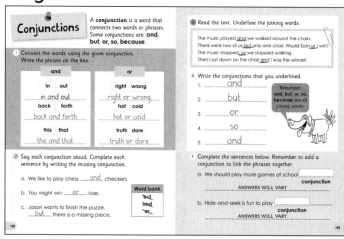

Page 104-105

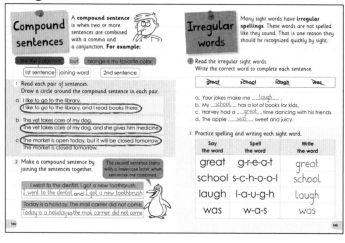

Page 106-107

Base words — A base word is a word that can stand alone. A base word can be changed by adding letters to the beginning or the end of the word.

1 Find and highlight the base word in yellow.

Base word	Highlight the base word	
wash	washing	rewash
play	playful	playing
hope	hoped	hopeful
call	recalled	calling
ring	ringing	rings
new	newest	renew

2 Draw a line to match each word to its base word.

Base word
fish — restful
quiet — runner
tie — fishing
rest — quietly
able — untie
run — unable

Inflectional endings — Inflectional endings are letters added to the end of a word to change its meaning. To add "ed" means something has already happened. To add "ing" means something is happening now.

1 Fill in the chart. Read each word aloud.

Base word	Add "ed" Past tense	Add "ing" Present tense
cook	cooked	cooking
jump	jumped	jumping
talk	talked	talking
clean	cleaned	cleaning

2 The inflectional ending "ed" can have many sounds. It can sound like /t/ in "looked." It can sound like /d/ in "played." It can sound like /id/ in "wanted." Read the word. Check the sound that you hear for "ed."

	/t/	/d/	/id/
fixed	/t/ ✓	/d/	/id/
loved	/t/	/d/ ✓	/id/
wanted	/t/	/d/	/id/ ✓
closed	/t/	/d/ ✓	/id/
waited	/t/	/d/	/id/ ✓
worked	/t/ ✓	/d/	/id/

Page 108-109

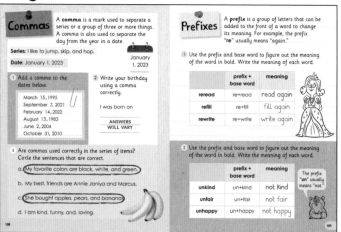

Page 110-111

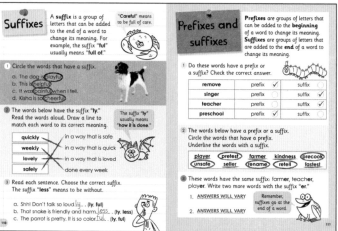